ISBN 0-8373-3667-8

C-3667 CAREER EXAMINATION SERIES

This is your PASSBOOK® for...

Employee Assistance Program Coordinator

Test Preparation Study Guide

Questions & Answers

NLC

NATIONAL LEARNING CORPORATION

Copyright © 2015 by

National Learning Corporation

212 Michael Drive, Syosset, New York 11791

All rights reserved, including the right of reproduction in whole or in part, in any form or by any means, electronic or mechanical, including photocopying, recording, or by any information storage and retrieval system, without permission in writing from the Publisher.

(516) 921-8888
(800) 645-6337
FAX: (516) 921-8743
www.passbooks.com
sales @ passbooks.com
info @ passbooks.com

PRINTED IN THE UNITED STATES OF AMERICA

PASSBOOK®
NOTICE

This book is SOLELY intended for, is sold ONLY to, and its use is RESTRICTED to *individual*, bona fide applicants or candidates who qualify by virtue of having seriously filed applications for appropriate license, certificate, professional and/or promotional advancement, higher school matriculation, scholarship, or other legitimate requirements of educational and/or governmental authorities.

This book is NOT intended for use, class instruction, tutoring, training, duplication, copying, reprinting, excerption, or adaptation, etc., by:

(1) Other publishers

(2) Proprietors and/or Instructors of "Coaching" and/or Preparatory Courses

(3) Personnel and/or Training Divisions of commercial, industrial, and governmental organizations

(4) Schools, colleges, or universities and/or their departments and staffs, including teachers and other personnel

(5) Testing Agencies or Bureaus

(6) Study groups which seek by the purchase of a single volume to copy and/or duplicate and/or adapt this material for use by the group as a whole without having purchased individual volumes for each of the members of the group

(7) Et al.

Such persons would be in violation of appropriate Federal and State statutes.

PROVISION OF LICENSING AGREEMENTS. — Recognized educational commercial, industrial, and governmental institutions and organizations, and others legitimately engaged in educational pursuits, including training, testing, and measurement activities, may address a request for a licensing agreement to the copyright owners, who will determine whether, and under what conditions, including fees and charges, the materials in this book may be used by them. In other words, a licensing facility exists for the legitimate use of the material in this book on other than an individual basis. However, it is asseverated and affirmed here that the material in this book *CANNOT* be used without the receipt of the express permission of such a licensing agreement from the Publishers.

NATIONAL LEARNING CORPORATION
212 Michael Drive
Syosset, New York 11791

Inquiries re licensing agreements should be addressed to:
The President
National Learning Corporation
212 Michael Drive
Syosset, New York 11791

PASSBOOK® SERIES

THE *PASSBOOK® SERIES* has been created to prepare applicants and candidates for the ultimate academic battlefield — the examination room.

At some time in our lives, each and every one of us may be required to take an examination — for validation, matriculation, admission, qualification, registration, certification, or licensure.

Based on the assumption that every applicant or candidate has met the basic formal educational standards, has taken the required number of courses, and read the necessary texts, the *PASSBOOK® SERIES* furnishes the one special preparation which may assure passing with confidence, instead of failing with insecurity. Examination questions — together with answers — are furnished as the basic vehicle for study so that the mysteries of the examination and its compounding difficulties may be eliminated or diminished by a sure method.

This book is meant to help you pass your examination provided that you qualify and are serious in your objective.

The entire field is reviewed through the huge store of content information which is succinctly presented through a provocative and challenging approach — the question-and-answer method.

A climate of success is established by furnishing the correct answers at the end of each test.

You soon learn to recognize types of questions, forms of questions, and patterns of questioning. You may even begin to anticipate expected outcomes.

You perceive that many questions are repeated or adapted so that you can gain acute insights, which may enable you to score many sure points.

You learn how to confront new questions, or types of questions, and to attack them confidently and work out the correct answers.

You note objectives and emphases, and recognize pitfalls and dangers, so that you may make positive educational adjustments.

Moreover, you are kept fully informed in relation to new concepts, methods, practices, and directions in the field.

You discover that you are actually taking the examination all the time: you are preparing for the examination by "taking" an examination, not by reading extraneous and/or supererogatory textbooks.

In short, this PASSBOOK®, used directedly, should be an important factor in helping you to pass your test.

EMPLOYEE ASSISTANCE PROGRAM COORDINATOR

DUTIES
Operates an Employee Assistance Program (EAP) within a municipality or other local jurisdiction. Provides direct assessment and referral services to the employees of that jurisdiction; may evaluate mental health treatment professionals, programs and agencies; promotes community awareness of services being offered. Performs related work as required.

SCOPE OF THE EXAMINATION
The written test will be designed to test for knowledge, skills, and/or abilities in such areas as:
1. Interviewing;
2. Assessment and referral of troubled employees;
3. Preparing written material;
4. Characteristics and problems of alcohol and substance abuse clients; and
5. Individual and group counseling.

HOW TO TAKE A TEST

I. YOU MUST PASS AN EXAMINATION

A. WHAT EVERY CANDIDATE SHOULD KNOW

Examination applicants often ask us for help in preparing for the written test. What can I study in advance? What kinds of questions will be asked? How will the test be given? How will the papers be graded?

As an applicant for a civil service examination, you may be wondering about some of these things. Our purpose here is to suggest effective methods of advance study and to describe civil service examinations.

Your chances for success on this examination can be increased if you know how to prepare. Those "pre-examination jitters" can be reduced if you know what to expect. You can even experience an adventure in good citizenship if you know why civil service exams are given.

B. WHY ARE CIVIL SERVICE EXAMINATIONS GIVEN?

Civil service examinations are important to you in two ways. As a citizen, you want public jobs filled by employees who know how to do their work. As a job seeker, you want a fair chance to compete for that job on an equal footing with other candidates. The best-known means of accomplishing this two-fold goal is the competitive examination.

Exams are widely publicized throughout the nation. They may be administered for jobs in federal, state, city, municipal, town or village governments or agencies.

Any citizen may apply, with some limitations, such as the age or residence of applicants. Your experience and education may be reviewed to see whether you meet the requirements for the particular examination. When these requirements exist, they are reasonable and applied consistently to all applicants. Thus, a competitive examination may cause you some uneasiness now, but it is your privilege and safeguard.

C. HOW ARE CIVIL SERVICE EXAMS DEVELOPED?

Examinations are carefully written by trained technicians who are specialists in the field known as "psychological measurement," in consultation with recognized authorities in the field of work that the test will cover. These experts recommend the subject matter areas or skills to be tested; only those knowledges or skills important to your success on the job are included. The most reliable books and source materials available are used as references. Together, the experts and technicians judge the difficulty level of the questions.

Test technicians know how to phrase questions so that the problem is clearly stated. Their ethics do not permit "trick" or "catch" questions. Questions may have been tried out on sample groups, or subjected to statistical analysis, to determine their usefulness.

Written tests are often used in combination with performance tests, ratings of training and experience, and oral interviews. All of these measures combine to form the best-known means of finding the right person for the right job.

II. HOW TO PASS THE WRITTEN TEST

A. NATURE OF THE EXAMINATION

To prepare intelligently for civil service examinations, you should know how they differ from school examinations you have taken. In school you were assigned certain definite pages to read or subjects to cover. The examination questions were quite detailed and usually emphasized memory. Civil service exams, on the other hand, try to discover your present ability to perform the duties of a position, plus your potentiality to learn these duties. In other words, a civil service exam attempts to predict how successful you will be. Questions cover such a broad area that they cannot be as minute and detailed as school exam questions.

In the public service similar kinds of work, or positions, are grouped together in one "class." This process is known as *position-classification*. All the positions in a class are paid according to the salary range for that class. One class title covers all of these positions, and they are all tested by the same examination.

B. FOUR BASIC STEPS

1) Study the announcement

How, then, can you know what subjects to study? Our best answer is: "Learn as much as possible about the class of positions for which you've applied." The exam will test the knowledge, skills and abilities needed to do the work.

Your most valuable source of information about the position you want is the official exam announcement. This announcement lists the training and experience qualifications. Check these standards and apply only if you come reasonably close to meeting them.

The brief description of the position in the examination announcement offers some clues to the subjects which will be tested. Think about the job itself. Review the duties in your mind. Can you perform them, or are there some in which you are rusty? Fill in the blank spots in your preparation.

Many jurisdictions preview the written test in the exam announcement by including a section called "Knowledge and Abilities Required," "Scope of the Examination," or some similar heading. Here you will find out specifically what fields will be tested.

2) Review your own background

Once you learn in general what the position is all about, and what you need to know to do the work, ask yourself which subjects you already know fairly well and which need improvement. You may wonder whether to concentrate on improving your strong areas or on building some background in your fields of weakness. When the announcement has specified "some knowledge" or "considerable knowledge," or has used adjectives like "beginning principles of…" or "advanced … methods," you can get a clue as to the number and difficulty of questions to be asked in any given field. More questions, and hence broader coverage, would be included for those subjects which are more important in the work. Now weigh your strengths and weaknesses against the job requirements and prepare accordingly.

3) Determine the level of the position

Another way to tell how intensively you should prepare is to understand the level of the job for which you are applying. Is it the entering level? In other words, is this the position in which beginners in a field of work are hired? Or is it an intermediate or advanced level? Sometimes this is indicated by such words as "Junior" or "Senior" in the class title. Other jurisdictions use Roman numerals to designate the level – Clerk I, Clerk II, for example. The word "Supervisor" sometimes appears in the title. If the level is not indicated by the title, check the description of duties. Will you be working under very close supervision, or will you have responsibility for independent decisions in this work?

4) Choose appropriate study materials

Now that you know the subjects to be examined and the relative amount of each subject to be covered, you can choose suitable study materials. For beginning level jobs, or even advanced ones, if you have a pronounced weakness in some aspect of your training, read a modern, standard textbook in that field. Be sure it is up to date and has general coverage. Such books are normally available at your library, and the librarian will be glad to help you locate one. For entry-level positions, questions of appropriate difficulty are chosen – neither highly advanced questions, nor those too simple. Such questions require careful thought but not advanced training.

If the position for which you are applying is technical or advanced, you will read more advanced, specialized material. If you are already familiar with the basic principles of your field, elementary textbooks would waste your time. Concentrate on advanced textbooks and technical periodicals. Think through the concepts and review difficult problems in your field.

These are all general sources. You can get more ideas on your own initiative, following these leads. For example, training manuals and publications of the government agency which employs workers in your field can be useful, particularly for technical and professional positions. A letter or visit to the government department involved may result in more specific study suggestions, and certainly will provide you with a more definite idea of the exact nature of the position you are seeking.

III. KINDS OF TESTS

Tests are used for purposes other than measuring knowledge and ability to perform specified duties. For some positions, it is equally important to test ability to make adjustments to new situations or to profit from training. In others, basic mental abilities not dependent on information are essential. Questions which test these things may not appear as pertinent to the duties of the position as those which test for knowledge and information. Yet they are often highly important parts of a fair examination. For very general questions, it is almost impossible to help you direct your study efforts. What we can do is to point out some of the more common of these general abilities needed in public service positions and describe some typical questions.

1) General information

Broad, general information has been found useful for predicting job success in some kinds of work. This is tested in a variety of ways, from vocabulary lists to questions about current events. Basic background in some field of work, such as sociology or economics, may be sampled in a group of questions. Often these are principles which have become familiar to most persons through exposure rather than through formal training. It is difficult to advise you how to study for these questions; being alert to the world around you is our best suggestion.

2) Verbal ability

An example of an ability needed in many positions is verbal or language ability. Verbal ability is, in brief, the ability to use and understand words. Vocabulary and grammar tests are typical measures of this ability. Reading comprehension or paragraph interpretation questions are common in many kinds of civil service tests. You are given a paragraph of written material and asked to find its central meaning.

3) Numerical ability
    Number skills can be tested by the familiar arithmetic problem, by checking paired lists of numbers to see which are alike and which are different, or by interpreting charts and graphs. In the latter test, a graph may be printed in the test booklet which you are asked to use as the basis for answering questions.

4) Observation
    A popular test for law-enforcement positions is the observation test. A picture is shown to you for several minutes, then taken away. Questions about the picture test your ability to observe both details and larger elements.

5) Following directions
    In many positions in the public service, the employee must be able to carry out written instructions dependably and accurately. You may be given a chart with several columns, each column listing a variety of information. The questions require you to carry out directions involving the information given in the chart.

6) Skills and aptitudes
    Performance tests effectively measure some manual skills and aptitudes. When the skill is one in which you are trained, such as typing or shorthand, you can practice. These tests are often very much like those given in business school or high school courses. For many of the other skills and aptitudes, however, no short-time preparation can be made. Skills and abilities natural to you or that you have developed throughout your lifetime are being tested.

    Many of the general questions just described provide all the data needed to answer the questions and ask you to use your reasoning ability to find the answers. Your best preparation for these tests, as well as for tests of facts and ideas, is to be at your physical and mental best. You, no doubt, have your own methods of getting into an exam-taking mood and keeping "in shape." The next section lists some ideas on this subject.

IV. KINDS OF QUESTIONS

    Only rarely is the "essay" question, which you answer in narrative form, used in civil service tests. Civil service tests are usually of the short-answer type. Full instructions for answering these questions will be given to you at the examination. But in case this is your first experience with short-answer questions and separate answer sheets, here is what you need to know:

1) Multiple-choice Questions
    Most popular of the short-answer questions is the "multiple choice" or "best answer" question. It can be used, for example, to test for factual knowledge, ability to solve problems or judgment in meeting situations found at work.
    A multiple-choice question is normally one of three types—
    - It can begin with an incomplete statement followed by several possible endings. You are to find the one ending which *best* completes the statement, although some of the others may not be entirely wrong.
    - It can also be a complete statement in the form of a question which is answered by choosing one of the statements listed.

- It can be in the form of a problem – again you select the best answer.

Here is an example of a multiple-choice question with a discussion which should give you some clues as to the method for choosing the right answer:

When an employee has a complaint about his assignment, the action which will *best* help him overcome his difficulty is to
    A. discuss his difficulty with his coworkers
    B. take the problem to the head of the organization
    C. take the problem to the person who gave him the assignment
    D. say nothing to anyone about his complaint

In answering this question, you should study each of the choices to find which is best. Consider choice "A" – Certainly an employee may discuss his complaint with fellow employees, but no change or improvement can result, and the complaint remains unresolved. Choice "B" is a poor choice since the head of the organization probably does not know what assignment you have been given, and taking your problem to him is known as "going over the head" of the supervisor. The supervisor, or person who made the assignment, is the person who can clarify it or correct any injustice. Choice "C" is, therefore, correct. To say nothing, as in choice "D," is unwise. Supervisors have and interest in knowing the problems employees are facing, and the employee is seeking a solution to his problem.

2) True/False Questions

The "true/false" or "right/wrong" form of question is sometimes used. Here a complete statement is given. Your job is to decide whether the statement is right or wrong.

SAMPLE: A roaming cell-phone call to a nearby city costs less than a non-roaming call to a distant city.

This statement is wrong, or false, since roaming calls are more expensive.
This is not a complete list of all possible question forms, although most of the others are variations of these common types. You will always get complete directions for answering questions. Be sure you understand *how* to mark your answers – ask questions until you do.

V. RECORDING YOUR ANSWERS

Computer terminals are used more and more today for many different kinds of exams.
For an examination with very few applicants, you may be told to record your answers in the test booklet itself. Separate answer sheets are much more common. If this separate answer sheet is to be scored by machine – and this is often the case – it is highly important that you mark your answers correctly in order to get credit.
An electronic scoring machine is often used in civil service offices because of the speed with which papers can be scored. Machine-scored answer sheets must be marked with a pencil, which will be given to you. This pencil has a high graphite content which responds to the electronic scoring machine. As a matter of fact, stray dots may register as answers, so do not let your pencil rest on the answer sheet while you are pondering the correct answer. Also, if your pencil lead breaks or is otherwise defective, ask for another.

Since the answer sheet will be dropped in a slot in the scoring machine, be careful not to bend the corners or get the paper crumpled.

The answer sheet normally has five vertical columns of numbers, with 30 numbers to a column. These numbers correspond to the question numbers in your test booklet. After each number, going across the page are four or five pairs of dotted lines. These short dotted lines have small letters or numbers above them. The first two pairs may also have a "T" or "F" above the letters. This indicates that the first two pairs only are to be used if the questions are of the true-false type. If the questions are multiple choice, disregard the "T" and "F" and pay attention only to the small letters or numbers.

Answer your questions in the manner of the sample that follows:

32. The largest city in the United States is
    A. Washington, D.C.
    B. New York City
    C. Chicago
    D. Detroit
    E. San Francisco

1) Choose the answer you think is best. (New York City is the largest, so "B" is correct.)
2) Find the row of dotted lines numbered the same as the question you are answering. (Find row number 32)
3) Find the pair of dotted lines corresponding to the answer. (Find the pair of lines under the mark "B.")
4) Make a solid black mark between the dotted lines.

VI. BEFORE THE TEST

Common sense will help you find procedures to follow to get ready for an examination. Too many of us, however, overlook these sensible measures. Indeed, nervousness and fatigue have been found to be the most serious reasons why applicants fail to do their best on civil service tests. Here is a list of reminders:

- Begin your preparation early – Don't wait until the last minute to go scurrying around for books and materials or to find out what the position is all about.
- Prepare continuously – An hour a night for a week is better than an all-night cram session. This has been definitely established. What is more, a night a week for a month will return better dividends than crowding your study into a shorter period of time.
- Locate the place of the exam – You have been sent a notice telling you when and where to report for the examination. If the location is in a different town or otherwise unfamiliar to you, it would be well to inquire the best route and learn something about the building.
- Relax the night before the test – Allow your mind to rest. Do not study at all that night. Plan some mild recreation or diversion; then go to bed early and get a good night's sleep.
- Get up early enough to make a leisurely trip to the place for the test – This way unforeseen events, traffic snarls, unfamiliar buildings, etc. will not upset you.
- Dress comfortably – A written test is not a fashion show. You will be known by number and not by name, so wear something comfortable.

- Leave excess paraphernalia at home – Shopping bags and odd bundles will get in your way. You need bring only the items mentioned in the official notice you received; usually everything you need is provided. Do not bring reference books to the exam. They will only confuse those last minutes and be taken away from you when in the test room.
- Arrive somewhat ahead of time – If because of transportation schedules you must get there very early, bring a newspaper or magazine to take your mind off yourself while waiting.
- Locate the examination room – When you have found the proper room, you will be directed to the seat or part of the room where you will sit. Sometimes you are given a sheet of instructions to read while you are waiting. Do not fill out any forms until you are told to do so; just read them and be prepared.
- Relax and prepare to listen to the instructions
- If you have any physical problem that may keep you from doing your best, be sure to tell the test administrator. If you are sick or in poor health, you really cannot do your best on the exam. You can come back and take the test some other time.

VII. AT THE TEST

The day of the test is here and you have the test booklet in your hand. The temptation to get going is very strong. Caution! There is more to success than knowing the right answers. You must know how to identify your papers and understand variations in the type of short-answer question used in this particular examination. Follow these suggestions for maximum results from your efforts:

1) Cooperate with the monitor

The test administrator has a duty to create a situation in which you can be as much at ease as possible. He will give instructions, tell you when to begin, check to see that you are marking your answer sheet correctly, and so on. He is not there to guard you, although he will see that your competitors do not take unfair advantage. He wants to help you do your best.

2) Listen to all instructions

Don't jump the gun! Wait until you understand all directions. In most civil service tests you get more time than you need to answer the questions. So don't be in a hurry. Read each word of instructions until you clearly understand the meaning. Study the examples, listen to all announcements and follow directions. Ask questions if you do not understand what to do.

3) Identify your papers

Civil service exams are usually identified by number only. You will be assigned a number; you must not put your name on your test papers. Be sure to copy your number correctly. Since more than one exam may be given, copy your exact examination title.

4) Plan your time

Unless you are told that a test is a "speed" or "rate of work" test, speed itself is usually not important. Time enough to answer all the questions will be provided, but this does not mean that you have all day. An overall time limit has been set. Divide the total time (in minutes) by the number of questions to determine the approximate time you have for each question.

5) Do not linger over difficult questions

If you come across a difficult question, mark it with a paper clip (useful to have along) and come back to it when you have been through the booklet. One caution if you do this — be sure to skip a number on your answer sheet as well. Check often to be sure that you have not lost your place and that you are marking in the row numbered the same as the question you are answering.

6) Read the questions

Be sure you know what the question asks! Many capable people are unsuccessful because they failed to *read* the questions correctly.

7) Answer all questions

Unless you have been instructed that a penalty will be deducted for incorrect answers, it is better to guess than to omit a question.

8) Speed tests

It is often better NOT to guess on speed tests. It has been found that on timed tests people are tempted to spend the last few seconds before time is called in marking answers at random – without even reading them – in the hope of picking up a few extra points. To discourage this practice, the instructions may warn you that your score will be "corrected" for guessing. That is, a penalty will be applied. The incorrect answers will be deducted from the correct ones, or some other penalty formula will be used.

9) Review your answers

If you finish before time is called, go back to the questions you guessed or omitted to give them further thought. Review other answers if you have time.

10) Return your test materials

If you are ready to leave before others have finished or time is called, take ALL your materials to the monitor and leave quietly. Never take any test material with you. The monitor can discover whose papers are not complete, and taking a test booklet may be grounds for disqualification.

VIII. EXAMINATION TECHNIQUES

1) Read the general instructions carefully. These are usually printed on the first page of the exam booklet. As a rule, these instructions refer to the timing of the examination; the fact that you should not start work until the signal and must stop work at a signal, etc. If there are any *special* instructions, such as a choice of questions to be answered, make sure that you note this instruction carefully.

2) When you are ready to start work on the examination, that is as soon as the signal has been given, read the instructions to each question booklet, underline any key words or phrases, such as *least*, *best*, *outline*, *describe* and the like. In this way you will tend to answer as requested rather than discover on reviewing your paper that you *listed without describing*, that you selected the *worst* choice rather than the *best* choice, etc.

3) If the examination is of the objective or multiple-choice type – that is, each question will also give a series of possible answers: A, B, C or D, and you are called upon to select the best answer and write the letter next to that answer on your answer paper – it is advisable to start answering each question in turn. There may be anywhere from 50 to 100 such questions in the three or four hours allotted and you can see how much time would be taken if you read through all the questions before beginning to answer any. Furthermore, if you come across a question or group of questions which you know would be difficult to answer, it would undoubtedly affect your handling of all the other questions.

4) If the examination is of the essay type and contains but a few questions, it is a moot point as to whether you should read all the questions before starting to answer any one. Of course, if you are given a choice – say five out of seven and the like – then it is essential to read all the questions so you can eliminate the two that are most difficult. If, however, you are asked to answer all the questions, there may be danger in trying to answer the easiest one first because you may find that you will spend too much time on it. The best technique is to answer the first question, then proceed to the second, etc.

5) Time your answers. Before the exam begins, write down the time it started, then add the time allowed for the examination and write down the time it must be completed, then divide the time available somewhat as follows:
    - If 3-1/2 hours are allowed, that would be 210 minutes. If you have 80 objective-type questions, that would be an average of 2-1/2 minutes per question. Allow yourself no more than 2 minutes per question, or a total of 160 minutes, which will permit about 50 minutes to review.
    - If for the time allotment of 210 minutes there are 7 essay questions to answer, that would average about 30 minutes a question. Give yourself only 25 minutes per question so that you have about 35 minutes to review.

6) The most important instruction is to *read each question* and make sure you know what is wanted. The second most important instruction is to *time yourself properly* so that you answer every question. The third most important instruction is to *answer every question*. Guess if you have to but include something for each question. Remember that you will receive no credit for a blank and will probably receive some credit if you write something in answer to an essay question. If you guess a letter – say "B" for a multiple-choice question – you may have guessed right. If you leave a blank as an answer to a multiple-choice question, the examiners may respect your feelings but it will not add a point to your score. Some exams may penalize you for wrong answers, so in such cases *only*, you may not want to guess unless you have some basis for your answer.

7) Suggestions
    a. Objective-type questions
        1. Examine the question booklet for proper sequence of pages and questions
        2. Read all instructions carefully
        3. Skip any question which seems too difficult; return to it after all other questions have been answered
        4. Apportion your time properly; do not spend too much time on any single question or group of questions

5. Note and underline key words – *all, most, fewest, least, best, worst, same, opposite,* etc.
6. Pay particular attention to negatives
7. Note unusual option, e.g., unduly long, short, complex, different or similar in content to the body of the question
8. Observe the use of "hedging" words – *probably, may, most likely,* etc.
9. Make sure that your answer is put next to the same number as the question
10. Do not second-guess unless you have good reason to believe the second answer is definitely more correct
11. Cross out original answer if you decide another answer is more accurate; do not erase until you are ready to hand your paper in
12. Answer all questions; guess unless instructed otherwise
13. Leave time for review

  b. Essay questions
    1. Read each question carefully
    2. Determine exactly what is wanted. Underline key words or phrases.
    3. Decide on outline or paragraph answer
    4. Include many different points and elements unless asked to develop any one or two points or elements
    5. Show impartiality by giving pros and cons unless directed to select one side only
    6. Make and write down any assumptions you find necessary to answer the questions
    7. Watch your English, grammar, punctuation and choice of words
    8. Time your answers; don't crowd material

8) Answering the essay question

Most essay questions can be answered by framing the specific response around several key words or ideas. Here are a few such key words or ideas:

M's: manpower, materials, methods, money, management
P's: purpose, program, policy, plan, procedure, practice, problems, pitfalls, personnel, public relations

  a. Six basic steps in handling problems:
    1. Preliminary plan and background development
    2. Collect information, data and facts
    3. Analyze and interpret information, data and facts
    4. Analyze and develop solutions as well as make recommendations
    5. Prepare report and sell recommendations
    6. Install recommendations and follow up effectiveness

  b. Pitfalls to avoid
    1. *Taking things for granted* – A statement of the situation does not necessarily imply that each of the elements is necessarily true; for example, a complaint may be invalid and biased so that all that can be taken for granted is that a complaint has been registered

2. *Considering only one side of a situation* – Wherever possible, indicate several alternatives and then point out the reasons you selected the best one
3. *Failing to indicate follow up* – Whenever your answer indicates action on your part, make certain that you will take proper follow-up action to see how successful your recommendations, procedures or actions turn out to be
4. *Taking too long in answering any single question* – Remember to time your answers properly

IX. AFTER THE TEST

Scoring procedures differ in detail among civil service jurisdictions although the general principles are the same. Whether the papers are hand-scored or graded by machine we have described, they are nearly always graded by number. That is, the person who marks the paper knows only the number – never the name – of the applicant. Not until all the papers have been graded will they be matched with names. If other tests, such as training and experience or oral interview ratings have been given, scores will be combined. Different parts of the examination usually have different weights. For example, the written test might count 60 percent of the final grade, and a rating of training and experience 40 percent. In many jurisdictions, veterans will have a certain number of points added to their grades.

After the final grade has been determined, the names are placed in grade order and an eligible list is established. There are various methods for resolving ties between those who get the same final grade – probably the most common is to place first the name of the person whose application was received first. Job offers are made from the eligible list in the order the names appear on it. You will be notified of your grade and your rank as soon as all these computations have been made. This will be done as rapidly as possible.

People who are found to meet the requirements in the announcement are called "eligibles." Their names are put on a list of eligible candidates. An eligible's chances of getting a job depend on how high he stands on this list and how fast agencies are filling jobs from the list.

When a job is to be filled from a list of eligibles, the agency asks for the names of people on the list of eligibles for that job. When the civil service commission receives this request, it sends to the agency the names of the three people highest on this list. Or, if the job to be filled has specialized requirements, the office sends the agency the names of the top three persons who meet these requirements from the general list.

The appointing officer makes a choice from among the three people whose names were sent to him. If the selected person accepts the appointment, the names of the others are put back on the list to be considered for future openings.

That is the rule in hiring from all kinds of eligible lists, whether they are for typist, carpenter, chemist, or something else. For every vacancy, the appointing officer has his choice of any one of the top three eligibles on the list. This explains why the person whose name is on top of the list sometimes does not get an appointment when some of the persons lower on the list do. If the appointing officer chooses the second or third eligible, the No. 1 eligible does not get a job at once, but stays on the list until he is appointed or the list is terminated.

X. HOW TO PASS THE INTERVIEW TEST

The examination for which you applied requires an oral interview test. You have already taken the written test and you are now being called for the interview test – the final part of the formal examination.

You may think that it is not possible to prepare for an interview test and that there are no procedures to follow during an interview. Our purpose is to point out some things you can do in advance that will help you and some good rules to follow and pitfalls to avoid while you are being interviewed.

What is an interview supposed to test?

The written examination is designed to test the technical knowledge and competence of the candidate; the oral is designed to evaluate intangible qualities, not readily measured otherwise, and to establish a list showing the relative fitness of each candidate – as measured against his competitors – for the position sought. Scoring is not on the basis of "right" and "wrong," but on a sliding scale of values ranging from "not passable" to "outstanding." As a matter of fact, it is possible to achieve a relatively low score without a single "incorrect" answer because of evident weakness in the qualities being measured.

Occasionally, an examination may consist entirely of an oral test – either an individual or a group oral. In such cases, information is sought concerning the technical knowledges and abilities of the candidate, since there has been no written examination for this purpose. More commonly, however, an oral test is used to supplement a written examination.

Who conducts interviews?

The composition of oral boards varies among different jurisdictions. In nearly all, a representative of the personnel department serves as chairman. One of the members of the board may be a representative of the department in which the candidate would work. In some cases, "outside experts" are used, and, frequently, a businessman or some other representative of the general public is asked to serve. Labor and management or other special groups may be represented. The aim is to secure the services of experts in the appropriate field.

However the board is composed, it is a good idea (and not at all improper or unethical) to ascertain in advance of the interview who the members are and what groups they represent. When you are introduced to them, you will have some idea of their backgrounds and interests, and at least you will not stutter and stammer over their names.

What should be done before the interview?

While knowledge about the board members is useful and takes some of the surprise element out of the interview, there is other preparation which is more substantive. It *is* possible to prepare for an oral interview – in several ways:

1) Keep a copy of your application and review it carefully before the interview

This may be the only document before the oral board, and the starting point of the interview. Know what education and experience you have listed there, and the sequence and dates of all of it. Sometimes the board will ask you to review the highlights of your experience for them; you should not have to hem and haw doing it.

2) Study the class specification and the examination announcement

Usually, the oral board has one or both of these to guide them. The qualities, characteristics or knowledges required by the position sought are stated in these documents. They offer valuable clues as to the nature of the oral interview. For example, if the job involves supervisory responsibilities, the announcement will usually indicate that knowledge of modern supervisory methods and the qualifications of the candidate as a supervisor will be tested. If so, you can expect such questions, frequently in the form of a hypothetical situation which you are expected to solve. NEVER go into an oral without knowledge of the duties and responsibilities of the job you seek.

3) Think through each qualification required
Try to visualize the kind of questions you would ask if you were a board member. How well could you answer them? Try especially to appraise your own knowledge and background in each area, *measured against the job sought*, and identify any areas in which you are weak. Be critical and realistic – do not flatter yourself.

4) Do some general reading in areas in which you feel you may be weak
For example, if the job involves supervision and your past experience has NOT, some general reading in supervisory methods and practices, particularly in the field of human relations, might be useful. Do NOT study agency procedures or detailed manuals. The oral board will be testing your understanding and capacity, not your memory.

5) Get a good night's sleep and watch your general health and mental attitude
You will want a clear head at the interview. Take care of a cold or any other minor ailment, and of course, no hangovers.

What should be done on the day of the interview?
Now comes the day of the interview itself. Give yourself plenty of time to get there. Plan to arrive somewhat ahead of the scheduled time, particularly if your appointment is in the fore part of the day. If a previous candidate fails to appear, the board might be ready for you a bit early. By early afternoon an oral board is almost invariably behind schedule if there are many candidates, and you may have to wait. Take along a book or magazine to read, or your application to review, but leave any extraneous material in the waiting room when you go in for your interview. In any event, relax and compose yourself.

The matter of dress is important. The board is forming impressions about you – from your experience, your manners, your attitude, and your appearance. Give your personal appearance careful attention. Dress your best, but not your flashiest. Choose conservative, appropriate clothing, and be sure it is immaculate. This is a business interview, and your appearance should indicate that you regard it as such. Besides, being well groomed and properly dressed will help boost your confidence.

Sooner or later, someone will call your name and escort you into the interview room. *This is it.* From here on you are on your own. It is too late for any more preparation. But remember, you asked for this opportunity to prove your fitness, and you are here because your request was granted.

What happens when you go in?
The usual sequence of events will be as follows: The clerk (who is often the board stenographer) will introduce you to the chairman of the oral board, who will introduce you to the other members of the board. Acknowledge the introductions before you sit down. Do not be surprised if you find a microphone facing you or a stenotypist sitting by. Oral interviews are usually recorded in the event of an appeal or other review.

Usually the chairman of the board will open the interview by reviewing the highlights of your education and work experience from your application – primarily for the benefit of the other members of the board, as well as to get the material into the record. Do not interrupt or comment unless there is an error or significant misinterpretation; if that is the case, do not hesitate. But do not quibble about insignificant matters. Also, he will usually ask you some question about your education, experience or your present job – partly to get you to start talking and to establish the interviewing "rapport." He may start the actual questioning, or turn it over to one of the other members. Frequently, each member undertakes the questioning on a particular area, one in which he is perhaps most competent, so you can expect each member to participate in the examination. Because time is limited, you may also expect some rather abrupt switches in the direction the questioning takes, so do not be upset by it. Normally, a board member will not pursue a single line of questioning unless he discovers a particular strength or weakness.

After each member has participated, the chairman will usually ask whether any member has any further questions, then will ask you if you have anything you wish to add. Unless you are expecting this question, it may floor you. Worse, it may start you off on an extended, extemporaneous speech. The board is not usually seeking more information. The question is principally to offer you a last opportunity to present further qualifications or to indicate that you have nothing to add. So, if you feel that a significant qualification or characteristic has been overlooked, it is proper to point it out in a sentence or so. Do not compliment the board on the thoroughness of their examination – they have been sketchy, and you know it. If you wish, merely say, "No thank you, I have nothing further to add." This is a point where you can "talk yourself out" of a good impression or fail to present an important bit of information. Remember, *you close the interview yourself.*

The chairman will then say, "That is all, Mr. _____, thank you." Do not be startled; the interview is over, and quicker than you think. Thank him, gather your belongings and take your leave. Save your sigh of relief for the other side of the door.

How to put your best foot forward

Throughout this entire process, you may feel that the board individually and collectively is trying to pierce your defenses, seek out your hidden weaknesses and embarrass and confuse you. Actually, this is not true. They are obliged to make an appraisal of your qualifications for the job you are seeking, and they want to see you in your best light. Remember, they must interview all candidates and a non-cooperative candidate may become a failure in spite of their best efforts to bring out his qualifications. Here are 15 suggestions that will help you:

1) Be natural – Keep your attitude confident, not cocky

If you are not confident that you can do the job, do not expect the board to be. Do not apologize for your weaknesses, try to bring out your strong points. The board is interested in a positive, not negative, presentation. Cockiness will antagonize any board member and make him wonder if you are covering up a weakness by a false show of strength.

2) Get comfortable, but don't lounge or sprawl

Sit erectly but not stiffly. A careless posture may lead the board to conclude that you are careless in other things, or at least that you are not impressed by the importance of the occasion. Either conclusion is natural, even if incorrect. Do not fuss with your clothing, a pencil or an ashtray. Your hands may occasionally be useful to emphasize a point; do not let them become a point of distraction.

3) Do not wisecrack or make small talk

This is a serious situation, and your attitude should show that you consider it as such. Further, the time of the board is limited – they do not want to waste it, and neither should you.

4) Do not exaggerate your experience or abilities

In the first place, from information in the application or other interviews and sources, the board may know more about you than you think. Secondly, you probably will not get away with it. An experienced board is rather adept at spotting such a situation, so do not take the chance.

5) If you know a board member, do not make a point of it, yet do not hide it

Certainly you are not fooling him, and probably not the other members of the board. Do not try to take advantage of your acquaintanceship – it will probably do you little good.

6) Do not dominate the interview

Let the board do that. They will give you the clues – do not assume that you have to do all the talking. Realize that the board has a number of questions to ask you, and do not try to take up all the interview time by showing off your extensive knowledge of the answer to the first one.

7) Be attentive

You only have 20 minutes or so, and you should keep your attention at its sharpest throughout. When a member is addressing a problem or question to you, give him your undivided attention. Address your reply principally to him, but do not exclude the other board members.

8) Do not interrupt

A board member may be stating a problem for you to analyze. He will ask you a question when the time comes. Let him state the problem, and wait for the question.

9) Make sure you understand the question

Do not try to answer until you are sure what the question is. If it is not clear, restate it in your own words or ask the board member to clarify it for you. However, do not haggle about minor elements.

10) Reply promptly but not hastily

A common entry on oral board rating sheets is "candidate responded readily," or "candidate hesitated in replies." Respond as promptly and quickly as you can, but do not jump to a hasty, ill-considered answer.

11) Do not be peremptory in your answers

A brief answer is proper – but do not fire your answer back. That is a losing game from your point of view. The board member can probably ask questions much faster than you can answer them.

12) Do not try to create the answer you think the board member wants

He is interested in what kind of mind you have and how it works – not in playing games. Furthermore, he can usually spot this practice and will actually grade you down on it.

13) Do not switch sides in your reply merely to agree with a board member

Frequently, a member will take a contrary position merely to draw you out and to see if you are willing and able to defend your point of view. Do not start a debate, yet do not surrender a good position. If a position is worth taking, it is worth defending.

14) Do not be afraid to admit an error in judgment if you are shown to be wrong

The board knows that you are forced to reply without any opportunity for careful consideration. Your answer may be demonstrably wrong. If so, admit it and get on with the interview.

15) Do not dwell at length on your present job

The opening question may relate to your present assignment. Answer the question but do not go into an extended discussion. You are being examined for a *new* job, not your present one. As a matter of fact, try to phrase ALL your answers in terms of the job for which you are being examined.

Basis of Rating

Probably you will forget most of these "do's" and "don'ts" when you walk into the oral interview room. Even remembering them all will not ensure you a passing grade. Perhaps you did not have the qualifications in the first place. But remembering them will help you to put your best foot forward, without treading on the toes of the board members.

Rumor and popular opinion to the contrary notwithstanding, an oral board wants you to make the best appearance possible. They know you are under pressure – but they also want to see how you respond to it as a guide to what your reaction would be under the pressures of the job you seek. They will be influenced by the degree of poise you display, the personal traits you show and the manner in which you respond.

ABOUT THIS BOOK

This book contains tests divided into Examination Sections. Go through each test, answering every question in the margin. We have also attached a sample answer sheet at the back of the book that can be removed and used. At the end of each test look at the answer key and check your answers. On the ones you got wrong, look at the right answer choice and learn. Do not fill in the answers first. Do not memorize the questions and answers, but understand the answer and principles involved. On your test, the questions will likely be different from the samples. Questions are changed and new ones added. If you understand these past questions you should have success with any changes that arise. Tests may consist of several types of questions. We have additional books on each subject should more study be advisable or necessary for you. Finally, the more you study, the better prepared you will be. This book is intended to be the last thing you study before you walk into the examination room. Prior study of relevant texts is also recommended. NLC publishes some of these in our Fundamental Series. Knowledge and good sense are important factors in passing your exam. Good luck also helps. So now study this Passbook, absorb the material contained within and take that knowledge into the examination. Then do your best to pass that exam.

EXAMINATION SECTION

EXAMINATION SECTION
TEST 1

DIRECTIONS: Each question or incomplete statement is followed by several suggested answers or completions. Select the one that BEST answers the question or completes the statement. *PRINT THE LETTER OF THE CORRECT ANSWER IN THE SPACE AT THE RIGHT.*

1. Deviant behavior is a sociological term used to describe behavior which is not in accord with generally accepted standards. This may include juvenile delinquency, adult criminality, mental or physical illness.
Comparison of normal with deviant behavior is useful to social workers because it

   A. makes it possible to establish watertight behavioral descriptions
   B. provides evidence of differential social behavior which distinguishes deviant from normal behavior
   C. indicates that deviant behavior is of no concern to social workers
   D. provides no evidence that social role is a determinant of behavior

   1.____

2. Alcoholism may affect an individual client's ability to function as a spouse, parent, worker, and citizen.
A social worker's MAIN responsibility to a client with a history of alcoholism is to

   A. interpret to the client the causes of alcoholism as a disease syndrome
   B. work with the alcoholic's family to accept him as he is and stop trying to reform him
   C. encourage the family of the alcoholic to accept casework treatment
   D. determine the origins of his particular drinking problem, establish a diagnosis, and work out a treatment plan for him

   2.____

3. There is a trend to regard narcotic addiction as a form of illness for which the current methods of intervention have not been effective.
Research on the combination of social, psychological, and physical causes of addiction would indicate that social workers should

   A. oppose hospitalization of addicts in institutions
   B. encourage the addict to live normally at home
   C. recognize that there is no successful treatment for addiction and act accordingly
   D. use the existing community facilities differentially for each addict

   3.____

4. A study of social relationships among delinquent and non-delinquent youth has shown that

   A. delinquent youth generally conceal their true feelings and maintain furtive social contacts
   B. delinquents are more impulsive and vivacious than law-abiding boys
   C. non-delinquent youths diminish their active social relationships in order to sublimate any anti-social impulses
   D. delinquent and non-delinquent youths exhibit similar characteristics of impulsiveness and vivaciousness

   4.____

5. The one of the following which is the CHIEF danger of interpreting the delinquent behavior of a child in terms of morality *alone* when attempting to get at its causes is that

   A. this tends to overlook the likelihood that the causes of the child's actions are more than a negation of morality and involve varied symptoms of disturbance
   B. a child's moral outlook toward life and society is largely colored by that of his parents, thus encouraging parent-child conflict
   C. too careful a consideration of the moral aspects of the offense and of the child's needs may often negate the demands of justice in a case
   D. standards of morality may be of no concern to the delinquent and he may not realize the seriousness of his offenses

6. Experts in the field of personnel administration are generally agreed that an employee should not be under the immediate supervision of more than one supervisor. A certain worker, because of an emergency situation, divides his time equally between two limited caseloads on a prearranged time schedule. Each unit has a different supervisor, and the worker performs substantially the same duties in each caseload.
   The above statement is pertinent in this situation CHIEFLY because

   A. each supervisor, feeling that the cases in her unit should have priority, may demand too much of the worker's time
   B. the two supervisors may have different standards of work performance and may prefer different methods of doing the work
   C. the worker works part-time on each caseload and may not have full knowledge or control of the situation in either caseload
   D. the task of evaluating the worker's services will be doubled, with two supervisors instead of one having to rate his work

7. Experts in modern personnel management generally agree that employees on all job levels should be permitted to offer suggestions for improving work methods.
   Of the following, the CHIEF limitation of such suggestions is that they may, at times,

   A. be offered primarily for financial reward and not show genuine interest in improvement of work methods
   B. be directed towards making individual jobs easier
   C. be restricted by the employees' fear of radically changing the work methods favored by their supervisors
   D. show little awareness of the effects on the overall objectives and functions of the entire agency

8. Through the supervisory process and relationship, the supervisor is trying to help workers gain increased self-awareness.
   Of the following statements concerning this process, the one which is MOST accurate is:

   A. Self-awareness is developed gradually so that worker can learn to control his own reactions.
   B. Worker is expected to be introspective primarily for his own enlightenment.
   C. Supervisor is trying to help worker handle any emotional difficulties he may reveal.
   D. Worker is expected at the onset to share and determine with the supervisor what in his previous background makes it difficult for him to use certain ideas.

9. The one of the following statements concerning principles in the learning process which is LEAST accurate is:

   A. Some degree of regression on the part of the worker is usually natural in the process of development and this should be accepted by the supervisor.
   B. When a beginning worker shows problems, the supervisor should first handle this behavior as a personality difficulty.
   C. It has been found in the work training process that some degree of resistance is usually inevitable.
   D. The emotional content of work practice may tend to set up *blind spots* in workers.

10. Of the following, the one that represents the BEST basis for planning the content of a successful staff development program is the

    A. time available for meetings
    B. chief social problems of the community
    C. common needs of the staff workers as related to the situations with which they are dealing
    D. experimental programs conducted by other agencies

11. In planning staff development seminars, the MOST valuable topics for discussion are likely to be those selected from

    A. staff suggestions based on the staff's interest and needs
    B. topics recommended for consideration by professional organizations
    C. topics selected by the administration based on demonstrated limitations of staff skill and knowledge
    D. topics selected by the administration based on a combination of staff interest and objectivity evaluated staff needs

12. Staff meetings designed to promote professional staff development are MOST likely to achieve this goal when

    A. there is the widest participation among all staff members who attend the meetings
    B. participation by the most skilled and experienced staff members is predominant
    C. participation by selected staff members is planned before the meeting sessions
    D. supervisory personnel take major responsibility for participation

13. Assume that you are the leader of a conference attended by representatives of various city and private agencies. After the conference has been underway for a considerable time, you realize that the representative of one of these agencies has said nothing. It would generally be BEST for you to

    A. ask him if he would like to say anything
    B. ask the group a pertinent question that he would probably be best able to answer
    C. make no special effort to include him in the conversation
    D. address the next question you planned to ask to him directly

14. A member of a decision-making conference generally makes his BEST contribution to the conference when he

    A. compromises on his own point of view and accepts most of the points of other conference members
    B. persuades the conference to accept all or most of his points

C. persuades the conference to accept his major proposals but will yield on the minor ones
D. succeeds in integrating his ideas with the ideas of the other conference members

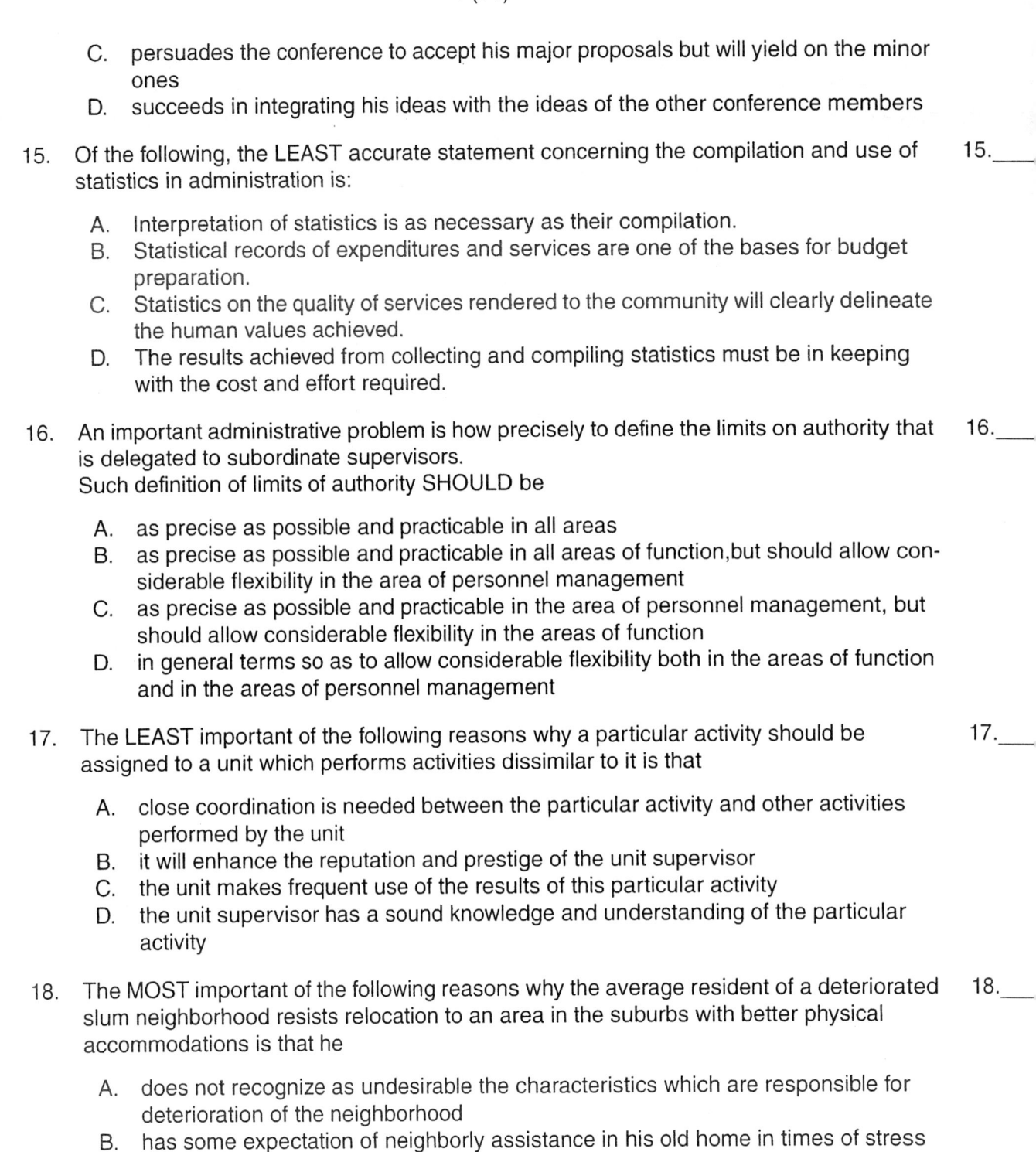

15. Of the following, the LEAST accurate statement concerning the compilation and use of statistics in administration is:

    A. Interpretation of statistics is as necessary as their compilation.
    B. Statistical records of expenditures and services are one of the bases for budget preparation.
    C. Statistics on the quality of services rendered to the community will clearly delineate the human values achieved.
    D. The results achieved from collecting and compiling statistics must be in keeping with the cost and effort required.

16. An important administrative problem is how precisely to define the limits on authority that is delegated to subordinate supervisors.
Such definition of limits of authority SHOULD be

    A. as precise as possible and practicable in all areas
    B. as precise as possible and practicable in all areas of function, but should allow considerable flexibility in the area of personnel management
    C. as precise as possible and practicable in the area of personnel management, but should allow considerable flexibility in the areas of function
    D. in general terms so as to allow considerable flexibility both in the areas of function and in the areas of personnel management

17. The LEAST important of the following reasons why a particular activity should be assigned to a unit which performs activities dissimilar to it is that

    A. close coordination is needed between the particular activity and other activities performed by the unit
    B. it will enhance the reputation and prestige of the unit supervisor
    C. the unit makes frequent use of the results of this particular activity
    D. the unit supervisor has a sound knowledge and understanding of the particular activity

18. The MOST important of the following reasons why the average resident of a deteriorated slum neighborhood resists relocation to an area in the suburbs with better physical accommodations is that he

    A. does not recognize as undesirable the characteristics which are responsible for deterioration of the neighborhood
    B. has some expectation of neighborly assistance in his old home in times of stress and adversity
    C. hopes for better days when he may be able to become a figure of some importance and envy in the old neighborhood
    D. is attuned to the noise of the city and fears the quiet of the suburb

19. From a psychological and sociological point of view, the MOST important of the following dangers to the persons living in an economically depressed area in which the only step taken by governmental and private social agencies to assist these persons is the granting of a dole is that

    A. industry will be reluctant to expand its operations in that area
    B. the dole will encourage additional non-producers to enter the area
    C. the residents of the area will probably have to find their own solution to their problems
    D. their permanent dependency will be fostered

20. The term *real wages* is GENERALLY used by economists to mean the

    A. amount of take-home pay left after taxes, social security, and other such deductions have been made by the employer
    B. average wage actually earned during a calendar or fiscal year
    C. family income expressed on a per capita basis
    D. wages expressed in terms of its buyer power

21. It has, at times, been suggested that an effective way to eradicate juvenile delinquency would be to arrest and punish the parents for the criminal actions of their delinquent children.
    The one of the following which is the CHIEF defect of this proposal is that

    A. it fails to get at the cause of the delinquent act and tends to further weaken disturbed parent-child relationships
    B. since the criminally inclined child has apparently demonstrated little love or affection for his parent, the child will be unlikely to amend his behavior in order to avoid hurting his parent
    C. the child who commits anti-social acts does so in many cases in order to hurt his parents so that this proposal would not only increase the parents' sorrow, but would also serve as an incentive to more delinquency by the child
    D. the punishment should be limited to the person who commits the illegal action rather than to those who are most interested in his welfare

22. Surveys which have compared the relative stability of marriages between white persons with marriages between non-white persons in this country have shown that, among Blacks, there is

    A. a significantly higher percentage of spouses absent from the household than among whites
    B. a significantly higher percentage of spouses absent from the household than among whites living in the South, but the opposite is true in the Northeast
    C. a significantly lower percentage of spouses absent from the household than among whites
    D. no significant difference in the percentage of spouses absent from the household when compared with the white population

23. A phenomenon found in the cultural and recreational patterns of European immigrant families in America is that, generally, the foreign-born adults

    A. as well as their children, tend soon to forget their old-world activities and adopt the cultural and recreational customs of America
    B. as well as their children, tend to retain and continue their old-world cultural and recreational pursuits, and find it equally difficult to adopt those of America
    C. tend soon to drop their old pursuits and adopt the cultural and recreational patterns of America while their children find it somewhat more difficult to make this change
    D. tend to retain and continue their old-world cultural and recreational pursuits while their children tend to rapidly replace these by the games and cultural patterns of America

23.____

24. Certain mores of migrant groups are strengthened under the impact of their contact with the native society while other mores are weakened.
In the case of Puerto Ricans who have come to the city, the effect of such contact upon their traditional family structure has been a

    A. strengthening of the former maternalistic family structure
    B. strengthening of the former paternalistic family structure
    C. weakening of the former maternalistic family structure
    D. weakening of the former paternalistic family structure

24.____

25. Administrative reviews and special studies of independent experts, as reported by the Department of Health, Education and Welfare, indicate that the proportion of recipients of public assistance who receive such assistance through *wilful misrepresentation* of the facts is

    A. less than 1%   B. about 4%
    C. between 4% and 7%   D. between 7% and 10%

25.____

KEY (CORRECT ANSWERS)

1.	B	11.	D
2.	D	12.	A
3.	D	13.	B
4.	B	14.	D
5.	A	15.	C
6.	B	16.	A
7.	D	17.	B
8.	A	18.	B
9.	B	19.	D
10.	C	20.	D

21. A
22. A
23. D
24. D
25. A

TEST 2

DIRECTIONS: Each question or incomplete statement is followed by several suggested answers or completions. Select the one that BEST answers the question or completes the statement. *PRINT THE LETTER OF THE CORRECT ANSWER IN THE SPACE AT THE RIGHT.*

1. In order to meet more adequately the public assistance needs occasioned by sudden changes in the national economy, social service agencies, in general, recommend, as a matter of preference, that

    A. each locality build up reserve funds to care for needy unemployed persons in order to avoid a breakdown of local resources such as occurred during the depression
    B. the federal government assume total responsibility for the administration of public assistance
    C. state settlement laws be strictly enforced so that unemployed workers will be encouraged to move from the emergency industry centers to their former homes
    D. a federal-state-local program of general assistance be established with need as the only eligibility requirement
    E. eligibility requirements be tightened to assure that only legitimately worthy local residents receive the available assistance

1._____

2. The MOST practical method of maintaining income for the majority of aged persons who are no longer able to work, or for the families of those workers who are deceased, is a(n)

    A. comprehensive system of non-categorical assistance on a basis of cash payments
    B. integrated system of public assistance and extensive work relief programs
    C. co-ordinated system of providing care in institutions and foster homes
    D. system of contributory insurance in which a cash benefit is paid as a matter of right
    E. expanded system of diagnostic and treatment centers

2._____

3. With the establishment of insurance and assistance programs under the Social Security Act, many institutional programs for the aged have tended to the greatest extent toward an increased emphasis on providing, of the following types of assistance,

    A. care for the aged by denominational groups
    B. care for children requiring institutional treatment
    C. recreational facilities for the able-bodied aged
    D. training facilities in industrial homework for the aged
    E. care for the chronically ill and infirm aged

3._____

4. Of the following terms, the one which BEST describes the Social Security Act is

    A. enabling legislation
    B. regulatory statute
    C. appropriations act
    D. act of mandamus
    E. provisional enactment

4._____

5. Of the following, the term which MOST accurately describes an appropriation is

   A. authority to spend
   B. itemized estimate
   C. *fund* accounting
   D. anticipated expenditure
   E. executive budget

6. When business expansion causes a demand for labor, the worker group which benefits MOST immediately is the group comprising

   A. employed workers
   B. inexperienced workers under 21 years of age
   C. experienced workers 21 to 25 years of age
   D. inexperienced older workers
   E. experienced workers over 40 years of age

7. The MOST important failure in our present system of providing social work services in local communities is the

   A. absence of adequate facilities for treating mental illness
   B. lack of coordination of available data and service in the community
   C. poor quality of the casework services provided by the public agencies
   D. limitations of the probation and parole services
   E. inadequacy of private family welfare services

8. Recent studies of the relationship between incidence of illness and the use of available treatment services among various population groups in the United States show that

   A. while lower-income families use medical services with greater frequency, total expenditures are greater among the upper-income groups
   B. although the average duration of a period of medical care increases with increasing income, the average frequency of obtaining care decreases with increasing income
   C. adequacy of medical service is inversely related to frequency of illness and size of family income
   D. families in the higher-income brackets have a heavier incidence of illness and make greater use of medical services than do those in the lower-income brackets
   E. both as to frequency and duration, the distribution of illness falls equally on all groups, but the use of medical services increases with income

9. The category of disease which most public health departments and authorities usually are NOT equipped to handle *directly* is that of

   A. chronic disease
   B. bronchial disturbances
   C. venereal disease
   D. mosquito-borne diseases
   E. incipient forms of tuberculosis

10. Recent statistical analyses of the causes of death in the United States indicate that medical science has now reached the stage where it would be preferable to increase its research toward control, among the following, PRINCIPALLY of

   A. accidents
   B. suicides
   C. communicable disease
   D. chronic disease
   E. infant mortality

10.____

11. Although the distinction between mental disease and mental deficiency is fairly definite, both these conditions USUALLY represent

   A. diseases of one part or organ of the body rather than of the whole person
   B. an inadequacy existing from birth or shortly afterwards and appearing as a simplicity of intelligence
   C. a deficiency developing later in life and characterized by distortions of attitude and belief
   D. inadequacies in meeting life situations and in conducting one's affairs
   E. somewhat transitory conditions characterized by disturbances of consciousness

11.____

12. According to studies made by reliable medical research organizations in the United States, differences among the states in proportion of physicians to population are MOST directly related to the

   A. geographic resources among the states
   B. skill of the physicians
   C. relative proportions of urban and rural people in the population of the states
   D. number of specialists in the ranks of the physicians
   E. health status of the people in the various states

12.____

13. One of the MAIN advantages of incorporating a charitable organization is that

   A. gifts or property of a corporation cannot be held in perpetuity
   B. gifts to unincorporated charitable organizations are not deductible from the taxable income
   C. incorporation gives less legal standing or *personality* than an informal partnership
   D. members of a corporation cannot be held liable for debts contracted by the organization
   E. a corporate organization cannot be sued

13.____

14. The BASIC principle underlying a social security program is that the government should provide

   A. aid to families that is not dependent on state or local participation
   B. assistance to any worthy family unable to maintain itself independently
   C. protection to individuals against some of the social risks that are inherent in an industrialized society
   D. safeguards against those factors leading to economic depression

14.____

4 (#2)

15. The activities of state and local public welfare agencies are dependent to a large degree on the public assistance program of the federal government.
The one of the following which the federal government has NOT been successful in achieving within the local agencies is the

   A. broadening of the scope of public assistance administration
   B. expansion of the categorical programs
   C. improvement of the quality of service given to clients
   D. standardization of the administration of general assistance programs

16. Of the following statements, the one which BEST describes the federal government's position, as stated in the Social Security Act, with regard to tests of character or fitness to be administered by local or state welfare departments to prospective clients is that

   A. no tests of character are required but they are not specifically prohibited
   B. if tests of character are used, they must be uniform throughout the state
   C. tests of character are contrary to the philosophy of the federal government and are to be considered illegal
   D. no tests of character are required, and assistance to those states that use them will be withheld

17. An increase in the size of the welfare grant may increase the cost of the welfare program not only in terms of those already on the welfare rolls, but because it may result in an increase in the number of people on the rolls.
The CHIEF reason that an increase in the size of the grant may cause an increase in the number of people on the rolls is that the increased grant may

   A. induce low-salaried wage earners to apply for assistance rather than continue at their menial jobs
   B. make eligible for assistance many people whose resources are just above the previous standard
   C. induce many people to apply for assistance who hesitated to do so because of meagerness of the previous grant
   D. make relatives less willing to contribute because the welfare grant can more adequately cover their dependents' needs

18. One of the MAIN differences between the use of casework methods by a public welfare agency and by a private welfare agency is that the public welfare agency

   A. requires that the applicant be eligible for the services it offers
   B. cannot maintain a non-judgmental attitude toward its clients because of legal requirements
   C. places less emphasis on efforts to change the behavior of its clients
   D. must be more objective in its approach to the client because public funds are involved

19. All definitions of social casework include certain major assumptions.
Of the following, the one which is NOT considered a major assumption is that

   A. the individual and society are interdependent
   B. social forces influence behavior and attitudes, affording opportunity for self-development and contribution to the world in which we live
   C. reconstruction of the total personality and reorganization of the total environment are specific goals
   D. the client is a responsible participant at every step in the solution of his problems

20. In order to provide those services to problem families which will help restore them to a self-maintaining status, it is necessary to FIRST   20._____

   A. develop specific plans to meet the individual needs of the problem family
   B. reduce the size of those caseloads composed of multi-problem families
   C. remove them from their environment and provide them with the means of overcoming their dependency
   D. identify the factors causing their dependency and creating problems for them

21. Of the following, the type of service which can provide the client with the MOST enduring help is that service which   21._____

   A. provides him with material aid and relieves the stress of his personal problems
   B. assists him to do as much as he can for himself and leaves him free to make his own decisions
   C. directs his efforts towards returning to a self-maintaining status and provides him with desirable goals
   D. gives him the feeling that the agency is interested in him as an individual and stands ready to assist him with his problems

22. Psychiatric interpretation of unconscious motivations can bring childhood conflicts into the framework of adult understanding and open the way for them to be resolved, but the interpretation must come from within the client.
    This statement means MOST NEARLY that   22._____

   A. treatment is merely diagnosis in reverse
   B. explaining a client to himself will lead to the resolution of his problems
   C. the client must arrive at an understanding of his problems
   D. unresolved childhood conflicts create problems for the adult

23. A significant factor in the United States economic picture is the state of the labor market. Of the following, the MOST important development affecting the labor market has been   23._____

   A. an expansion of the national defense effort creating new plant capacity
   B. the general increase in personal income as a result of an increase in overtime pay in manufacturing industries
   C. the growth of manufacturing as a result of automation
   D. a demand for a large number of jobs resulting from new job applicants as well as from displacement of workers by automation

24. A typical characteristic of the United States population over 65 is that MOST of them   24._____

   A. are independent and capable of self-support
   B. live in their own homes but require various supportive services
   C. live in institutions for the aged
   D. require constant medical attention at home or in an institution

25. The one of the following factors which is MOST important in preventing persons 65 years of age and older from getting employment is the   25._____

   A. misconceptions by employers of skills and abilities of senior citizens
   B. lack of skill in modern industrial techniques of persons in this age group
   C. social security laws restricting employment of persons in this age group
   D. unwillingness of persons in this age group to continue supporting themselves

KEY (CORRECT ANSWERS)

1.	D		11.	D
2.	D		12.	C
3.	E		13.	D
4.	A		14.	C
5.	A		15.	D
6.	B		16.	A
7.	B		17.	B
8.	C		18.	C
9.	A		19.	C
10.	D		20.	D

21. B
22. C
23. D
24. B
25. A

EXAMINATION SECTION
TEST 1

DIRECTIONS: Each question or incomplete statement is followed by several suggested answers or completions. Select the one that BEST answers the question or completes the statement. *PRINT THE LETTER OF THE CORRECT ANSWER IN THE SPACE AT THE RIGHT.*

1. Managing conflict effectively by avoiding no-win situations, positively influencing the actions of others and using _____ strategies are what make a great leader.

    A. persuasive
    B. ambiguous
    C. prosecution
    D. performance

    1._____

2. In today's business world, collaboration will bring together people from distinct backgrounds. These collaborative groups may not share common norms, morals or _____, but they can offer unique _____.

    A. vocabulary; perspectives
    B. salaries; vocabulary
    C. modifications; insights
    D. perspectives; salaries

    2._____

3. E-mail is a great tool for communication, however, which of the following should you be careful of when in electronic communication with a colleague?

    A. Font size
    B. E-mail length
    C. Font color
    D. Tone of voice

    3._____

4. A formal relationship can best be described as

    A. regulated by procedures or directives
    B. personal and relaxed
    C. emotionally distant and very uncomfortable
    D. confusing and unproductive

    4._____

5. John is in a meeting with his supervisor and coworkers. He is thinking about what he's going to have for dinner that night when his boss asks him a question. John can repeat back what his supervisor said, but he cannot retain what was said during the meeting. This is a classic example of failing to

    A. focus at work
    B. effectively listen
    C. leave personal plans outside the workplace
    D. care about meetings

    5._____

6. A person's choice of _____ can directly affect communication.

    A. clothing
    B. food
    C. hygiene
    D. words

7. Why is it important to relax when communicating with team members?

    A. Relaxing always means having better ideas
    B. People will automatically like you more if you are relaxed
    C. If you are nervous, you may talk too quickly and make it hard for others to understand your message or directive
    D. No one likes someone who is always working, so it is important to relax and not work too hard

8. In order to show you are genuinely interested in what others have to say, you should

    A. tell them how nice they are
    B. repeat what they say back to them
    C. nod and find something to compliment them about
    D. ask questions and seek clarification from them

9. Jack and James are always arguing with one another. Their supervisor calls each one in separately to talk to them. He asks Jack to think about things from James' point of view and he asks James to do the same for Jack. What is the supervisor trying to get each person to do?

    A. Get along
    B. Be positive
    C. Communicate effectively
    D. Empathize

10. When working in groups, disagreements

    A. should be avoided at all costs
    B. are often a healthy way of building understanding and camaraderie
    C. lead coworkers to hate one another and the company they work for
    D. don't happen if the supervisor chooses the right people to work together

11. If things go wrong in a group situation, it is important to AVOID

    A. the boss
    B. disagreements or arguments
    C. scapegoating
    D. being polite and fair to one another

12. If you are a listener who likes to hear the rationale behind a message, your listening style would be described as _____ style.   12._____

    A. results
    B. process
    C. reasons
    D. eye contact

13. Which of the following best describes a psychological barrier in communication?   13._____

    A. Molly is so stressed about her paying for her mortgage that she can't focus at work right now
    B. John doesn't understand a lot of the terms that the IT specialist used in an e-mail sent out to everyone
    C. Jerry is a little older and has a hard time hearing everything so sometimes he misses parts of a conversation
    D. Linda doesn't want to be at the company for longer than a few months, so she doesn't really try too hard to fit in

14. Body language, also known as _____, is really important when building rapport with coworkers and communicating effectively.   14._____

    A. verbal language
    B. kinesthetics
    C. non-verbal communication
    D. facial expressions

15. Which of the following might be a good example of someone who has a 'closed' posture?   15._____

    A. Hands are apart on the arms of the chair
    B. His/her arms are folded
    C. They are directly facing you
    D. They barely speak above a whisper

16. Which of the following can eye contact be used for?   16._____

    A. To give and receive feedback
    B. To let someone know when it is their turn to speak
    C. To communicate how you feel about someone
    D. All of the above

17. Which of the following is NOT a form of non-verbal communication?

    A. Crossing your arms when talking to someone
    B. Using space within the room in a conversation
    C. Clearing your throat before you speak
    D. Saying "10-4" when asked if you understand

18. Your best friend has just been hired at the company you work for. You notice he has come into work on several occasions after staying out late the night before. His work has not suffered yet, but you fear it will. Which of the following actions should you take to help prevent future problems?

    A. Do nothing; he's your friend but it is his life
    B. Try to talk to him and help him see the importance of not creating bad habits
    C. Talk to your supervisor and tell him your friend isn't suitable for the job
    D. Tell your friend to change his ways or to quit

19. Interacting with coworkers can be positively or negatively affected by _____, when someone's previous biases and assumptions shape their reactions in future situations.

    A. racism
    B. past experience
    C. interpersonal skills
    D. active listening

20. Which of the following scenarios BEST describes a person who is being subjective?

    A. Sally is fair and honest when she listens to coworkers. She does not take sides and wants the best solution to the problem.
    B. Mike doesn't like Steve, because he thinks Steve is only out for himself. Still, Steve offers valuable insights, so Mike tries not to let personal feelings get in the way of working together.
    C. Jamie is dating Veronica's ex and Veronica just found out. Now, Veronica immediately shoots down anything Jamie suggests during a meeting as irrational and superfluous.
    D. None of the above.

21. Which important communications term is most closely defined as "the quality of a sound governed by the rate of vibrations producing it; the degree of highness or lowness of a tone"?

    A. Tone   B. Pitch
    C. Effective communication   D. Rationalization

22. _____ is when a person tries to make an imprudent and reckless action seem reasonable. 22._____

   A. Projection
   B. Self-deception
   C. Past experience
   D. Rationalization

23. When holding conversations with coworkers, you should 23._____

   A. do most of the talking
   B. let others do most of the talking
   C. try to split time between talking and listening
   D. zone out and wait for the meeting to finish

24. A new hire just arrived and you are meeting her for the first time. Which of the following actions is most appropriate? 24._____

   A. Walk up and introduce yourself with a smile and a handshake
   B. Wait for her to come and introduce herself
   C. Approach her and offer a hug to make her feel welcome
   D. Ignore the new hire; she is likely your competition

25. If you are the type of listener who likes to discuss concepts or issues in detail, you would most likely fall under which listening style? 25._____

   A. Process
   B. Reasons
   C. Results
   D. None of the above

KEY (CORRECT ANSWERS)

1. A	11. C	21. B
2. A	12. C	22. D
3. D	13. A	23. C
4. A	14. C	24. A
5. B	15. B	25. A
6. D	16. D	
7. C	17. D	
8. D	18. B	
9. D	19. B	
10. B	20. C	

TEST 2

DIRECTIONS: Each question or incomplete statement is followed by several suggested answers or completions. Select the one that BEST answers the question or completes the statement. *PRINT THE LETTER OF THE CORRECT ANSWER IN THE SPACE AT THE RIGHT.*

1. Which of the following is an example of the best practice when communicating in the workplace?

    A. You are horrible with remembering names so you try to use nicknames to cover up for your poor memory
    B. You only pay attention to the names of people who you work for or who you deem to be "important"
    C. You try to remember everyone's names and use them whenever possible
    D. None of the above

    1._____

2. Words of civility such as "please" and "thank you" should be used _____ when conversing with coworkers and business partners.

    A. always
    B. sometimes
    C. rarely
    D. never

    2._____

3. When communicating with others, one should _____ stand as close to them as possible and make body contact in order to get an important point across.

    A. always
    B. sometimes
    C. rarely
    D. never

    3._____

4. The most appropriate way to end a conversation is to

    A. seek a mutual resolution, but leave abruptly if it continues
    B. find a way to wrap up the conversation so the other person knows it is time to move on
    C. look impatient so hopefully the person will get the hint
    D. tell the other person the conversation should end

    4._____

5. Another name for interpersonal communication in an office setting is

    A. peer-to-peer communication
    B. mass communication
    C. virtual reality
    D. e-mailing

    5._____

6. Of the following statements, choose the one you feel is the most correct.   6._____

   A. Devoid of interpersonal communication, people become sick
   B. Communication is not completely needed for humans
   C. People are the only animals that need to have relationships in order to survive
   D. Important communication is not really relevant until after you become an adult

7. John is giving a presentation on ways to communicate effectively with peers. He is having trouble deciding on what to say in his speech. Which of the following statements should he AVOID using?   7._____

   A. Always try to understand another person's point of view or perspective
   B. Try to imagine what someone is going to say before they actually say it
   C. Be aware of how non-verbal cues like eye contact and body language affect how your message is received
   D. Both B and C

8. Which of the following would MOST affect our perception of communication with coworkers?   8._____

   A. Past experiences
   B. Marital problems
   C. Rumors spread about coworkers
   D. None of the above

9. Many people think of communication as both _____ and _____ messages.   9._____

   A. formal; informal
   B. hearing; listening
   C. sending; receiving
   D. finding; decoding

10. Why is context important in communication?   10._____

    A. It's important to know which buttons to push in order to get what you want
    B. Saying something to one person may not have the same effect as saying it to someone else
    C. Context is only important if you are worried about what others think
    D. None of the above

11. If your brother is normally bright and talkative during the summer, but you notice he gets quiet and subdued in the winter, the most likely communication context he is dealing with would be

    A. relational
    B. cultural
    C. inner
    D. physical

11._____

12. _____ is an example of a negative nonverbal action you can take.

    A. Smiling
    B. Using a tone of voice that matches your message
    C. Maintaining eye contact
    D. Slumping your shoulders

12._____

13. Cultural context can best be described as

    A. what people think of as it relates to the event they are participating in (i.e. a wedding versus a funeral)
    B. the connection between a father and his son
    C. rules and patterns of Americans versus the Japanese
    D. thoughts, feelings and sensations inside a person's head

13._____

14. Which of the following BEST describes feedback?

    A. Staring at the speaker while he talks
    B. Nodding and smiling while listening to a speaker
    C. Standing an appropriate distance away so the speaker does not get uncomfortable
    D. Trying to speak while the other person is speaking because you have something more important to say

14._____

15. Being able to communicate more effectively can be improved upon by

    A. continually making an effort to be as flexible as possible when talking to others
    B. committing to one style of speaking until you master it
    C. using the same style of correspondence as the person with whom you are speaking
    D. always using the opposite style of communication from the person you are speaking to

15._____

16. John walks up to Sally and compliments her on the dress she wore to work today. In his mind, John was just being friendly, but Sally went to her manager and filed a harassment charge against John. This miscommunication could most easily be classified as an error in what?

16._____

A. Reality
B. Perception
C. Friendship
D. Loyalty

17. If a speaker's tone is flat and monotone, which of the following is the most likely reaction that listeners will have?   17._____

    A. They will be enthused by the message
    B. They will enjoy the message but not be overly excited about it
    C. They will be polite and interested but will not seem very engaged
    D. They will be bored and uninterested in the message

18. When Steve speaks to his group about his ideas, he generally has a higher pitch to his voice and gesticulates frequently. This leads his team members to believe that Steve   18._____

    A. is enthusiastic and has great ideas for the group
    B. has had too much caffeine and needs to relax
    C. is trying to show off for the boss and make them look bad
    D. is extremely smart and great at his job

19. _____ is used when a person wants to add stress to key words in communication. It lets the audience understand the mood or feelings of particular words or phrases.   19._____

    A. Anger
    B. Tone
    C. Perception
    D. Inflection

20. If Barry tells Bill that his haircut looks "great" and Bill can tell Barry is being insincere, which of the following tones is Barry most likely using?   20._____

    A. Affectionate
    B. Apologetic
    C. Threatening
    D. Sarcastic

21. As a supervisor, it is important that everyone clearly comprehends everything you communicate to them. In order to ensure this happens, which of the following things should you avoid?   21._____

    A. Overusing jargon
    B. Explaining something more than once
    C. Speaking slowly and annunciating everything
    D. Having meetings in the morning

22. If your supervisor is looking down at the ground or has his back to you as he is speaking, it most clearly indicates to those who are listening to him that the supervisor

    A. is shy and doesn't like speaking in front of people
    B. is disinterested and doesn't care what he's talking about
    C. is approachable and friendly
    D. dislikes his job and wants to get out as soon as possible

22._____

23. Interpersonal communication helps you

    A. know what others are thinking
    B. turn into an inspiring speaker, especially in public
    C. learn about yourself
    D. communicate with the general public

23._____

24. In general, people who smile more are perceived as

    A. devious   B. friendly
    C. attractive   D. easy to manipulate

24._____

25. If your supervisor constantly takes advantage of you and expresses his or her opinion often at the expense of you or other workers, which communication style are they most likely using?

    A. Nonassertive
    B. Assertive
    C. Aggressive
    D. Peacemaking

25._____

KEY (CORRECT ANSWERS)

1. C	11. D	21. A
2. A	12. D	22. B
3. D	13. C	23. D
4. B	14. B	24. B
5. A	15. A	25. C
6. A	16. B	
7. B	17. D	
8. A	18. A	
9. C	19. D	
10. B	20. D	

EXAMINATION SECTION
TEST 1

DIRECTIONS: Each question or incomplete statement is followed by several suggested answers or completions. Select the one that BEST answers the question or completes the statement. *PRINT THE LETTER OF THE CORRECT ANSWER IN THE SPACE AT THE RIGHT.*

1. When a counselee describes a problem which is similar to one the counselor has had, the counselor usually should

    A. tell the counselee how he reacted in similar circumstances
    B. suggest solutions which worked for him
    C. describe his own experiences, but disguise them by saying they happened to another of his counselees
    D. make no reference to his experience

2. Of the following, the MOST highly specialized process in guidance is

    A. testing   B. occupational study
    C. interviewing   D. counseling

3. Which of the following is the MOST fundamental aim of guidance?

    A. Solve client's problems
    B. Counsel clients concerning problems
    C. Develop self-direction
    D. Direct the client to strive for excellence

4. A counselor forecasts the extent to which the counselee may or may not make a desirable or satisfying adaptation to his situation. Williamson referred to this step in the counseling process as

    A. synthesis   B. prognosis
    C. follow-up   D. diagnosis

5. A fundamental assumption made by the client-centered school of counseling is that

    A. diagnosis is essential to effective counseling
    B. every individual possesses a "tendency toward growth"
    C. responsibility for client actions is assumed by the counselor
    D. the counselor's role is primarily one of giving information to the counselee

6. Referral of a client to other agencies should be made

    A. after a long period of counseling has proved ineffectual
    B. only with the client's and his parent's consent
    C. as soon as the needed adjustment lies outside of client's, as well as counselor's, control
    D. after consultation with teachers and administration

7. According to field theory, individuals who are initially faced with a problem tend to seek

   A. long involved indirect solutions
   B. simple direct solutions
   C. outside help in forcing a solution
   D. means of withdrawing from the problem

8. In regard to client activity, the goal of counseling agreed upon by all methodologies is

   A. integrated controlled behavior
   B. release of feeling and negative emotion
   C. more individuals who understand themselves
   D. conformity to the cultural mores

9. A counselor who is primarily concerned with analyzing and diagnosing a client's problems, collecting and synthesizing data about the client, and making predictions about the consequences of various client decisions would BEST be classified as using which method of counseling? The

   A. *clinical* method as described by Williamson
   B. *client-centered* method as described by Rogers
   C. *communications* method as described by Robinson
   D. *learning* method as described by Dollard & Miller

10. Most definitions would NOT include which of the following as a necessary aspect of counseling?

    A. The counselor and client meet face-to-face.
    B. The client is experiencing a degree of emotional disturbance.
    C. A unique learning opportunity is provided for the client.
    D. The counselor brings special competence to the counseling relationship.

11. The *initial* counseling interview is considered by many to be hardest.
    Which one of the following is NOT an essential objective of this session? To

    A. develop a sound working relationship with the individual
    B. make a diagnosis of the client's problem
    C. orient the client to the nature of the counseling process
    D. provide an atmosphere that allows the individual to express freely his attitudes and feelings

12. A powerful dynamic in the counseling process and usually the very antithesis of its counterpart in the instructional process is

    A. encouraging accuracy
    B. emphasizing structure
    C. encouraging sequential orderly thinking
    D. processing ambiguity

13. Counseling techniques are useful in working with advantaged, bright or creative children. Fundamental is a counseling atmosphere that is 13.____

    A. non-threatening
    B. urging for creativity
    C. highly charged to stimulate excitement
    D. pretty well structured

14. Which one of the following counseling approaches emphasizes differential diagnosis in the treatment of individual clients? 14.____

    A. Trait- and factor-centered
    B. Self-theory
    C. Communications
    D. Psychoanalytic

15. The school of counseling theory, characterized by the attempt to observe behavior from the point of view of the individual himself (i.e., his own frame of reference), is known as 15.____

    A. organismic   B. neo-Freudianism
    C. existentialism   D. phenomenology

16. Of the following, which characteristic do counseling theorists consider MOST essential to the effectiveness of a counselor? 16.____

    A. Extroversion   B. Persuasiveness
    C. Serenity   D. Objectivity

17. The counseling approach which uses any of a variety of techniques which BEST suit individual situations is called 17.____

    A. instinctive   B. specific
    C. conditioning   D. eclectic

18. Mental testing, statistics, and measurement are identified *most closely* with which one of the following counseling approaches? 18.____

    A. Neobehavioral   B. Trait- and factor-centered
    C. Psychoanalytic   D. Communications

19. The "self-actualization" process is the central tendency of which one of the following approaches in counseling? 19.____

    A. Neobehavioral   B. Communications
    C. Self-theory   D. Psychoanalytic

20. In counseling, the LEAST acceptable introduction in phrasing an interpretative statement is which one of the following? 20.____

    A. "It seems as though..."
    B. "Do you suppose that..."
    C. "It probably would be better if..."
    D. "I'm wondering if..."

21. The term "ambiguity" in counseling refers to the degree of, openness or uncertainty that exists in the minds of both counselor and client regarding what is supposed to happen next.
    The ULTIMATE degree of ambiguity in counseling is represented by the use of

    A. open-ended leads
    B. depth interpretation
    C. "yes" and "no" questions
    D. free association

22. The client says, "I can't seem to get along with the other kids."
    Of the following, the MOST appropriate counselor response is:

    A. "Have you done your part?"
    B. "Let's talk about it."
    C. "You're too reserved and too cold."
    D. "You don't care very much about it."

23. In psychoanalytically-oriented counseling, the responsibility for the client's bringing up and talking about important material lies

    A. *exclusively* with the client
    B. *primarily* with the client, with the help of the counselor
    C. *primarily* with the counselor, with the cooperation of the client
    D. *exclusively* with the counselor

24. Research shows that, regardless of theoretical persuasion, experienced counselors as compared with less experienced counselors tend to

    A. use a wider range of techniques
    B. rely primarily on reflection of feeling
    C. use deeper interpretations
    D. take more responsibility for content

25. STRUCTURING in counseling is the process of

    A. building rapport in the initial interview
    B. establishing the ground rules for the counselor
    C. determining the client's real problem
    D. communicating and sharing expectations about counseling

KEY (CORRECT ANSWERS)

1.	D		11.	B
2.	D		12.	D
3.	C		13.	A
4.	B		14.	A
5.	B		15.	D
6.	C		16.	D
7.	B		17.	D
8.	A		18.	B
9.	A		19.	C
10.	B		20.	C

21. D
22. B
23. B
24. A
25. D

TEST 2

DIRECTIONS: Each question or incomplete statement is followed by several suggested answers or completions. Select the one that BEST answers the question or completes the statement. *PRINT THE LETTER OF THE CORRECT ANSWER IN THE SPACE AT THE RIGHT.*

1. Of non-white youngsters in the United States who drop out before completing 4 years of high school, what proportion come from families earning less than $20,000?

    A. 25% B. 40% C. Over 50% D. Over 90%

2. Educational attainment has been rising. Median school years of attainment for persons now holding clerical or sales jobs average

    A. more than 12 years
    B. less than 12 years
    C. more than 10 years
    D. less than 10 years

3. From the client-centered point of view of counseling, information about the client's skills, personality, etc. are best used

    A. to help the counselor to understand the client better
    B. to help the client to understand himself better
    C. as a basis for the counselor's suggestions, which the client is free to reject
    D. as a part of the counselor's diagnosis in deciding how best to work with the client

4. Appropriate responses for a counselor include all of the following EXCEPT

    A. "If I were you..."
    B. "Can you tell me more about...?"
    C. "How do you feel about...?"
    D. "How long has this been going on...?"

5. During the early stages of a counseling relationship, a client engages in long periods of silence and appears to have difficulty in discussing questions which the counselor raises. A psychoanalytically-oriented counselor would *probably* interpret these silences and difficulties as signs of

    A. lack of rapport
    B. frustrated oral needs
    C. the client's inability to analyze his problems
    D. resistance to dealing with emotional problems

6. The single recent book which focuses specifically on problems of professionalization in counseling in the present society and makes dramatic recommendations for counselor training is THE COUNSELOR IN A CHANGING WORLD. The author is

    A. Dugald S. Arbuckle
    B. Edward C. Glanz
    C. Leslie E. Moser
    D. C. Gilbert Wrenn

7. All of above the following are identified with existential counseling EXCEPT

    A. Frankl
    B. May
    C. Van Kamm
    D. Eysenck

8. In the final analysis, realization of potential by the individual depends upon

   A. his abilities
   B. the limits imposed by his society and culture
   C. subjective interactional factors
   D. all of the above

9. Which one of the following is the MOST important deterrent to evaluation of guidance programs? Lack of

   A. objective data
   B. suitable criteria
   C. research skills among guidance workers
   D. data processing equipment

10. Acculturation, the process of acquiring values different from those of the culture into which one is born, can BEST be promoted through guidance of

    A. introducing the student to the new culture
    B. showing the student how the culture into which he was born is inadequate
    C. supporting the individual in learning the new culture and by rewarding him for the new learning
    D. showing the student that cultural differences are relatively unimportant

11. The client speaks so low that you cannot hear what he is saying.
    The BEST technique to use in handling this would be to

    A. confront the client with the problem
    B. pretend that you can hear him
    C. respond in like manner
    D. interpret this action to him as an "interpersonal defense mechanism"

12. All of the following are important in the "social-psychological" theories of counseling EXCEPT

    A. life style
    B. cognitive processes
    C. interpersonal relationships
    D. need for identity

13. In distinguishing between counseling and clinical psychology, which of the following tends to be TRUE of the counselor but not of the clinician?

    A. The major focus is on the normal, adaptive resources of the client's personality
    B. The use of psychological test data to contribute to a better understanding of the client
    C. A supportive and accepting relationship is developed
    D. The disintegrative, disturbed aspects of the client's personality receive major attention

14. Which of the following words is MOST similar in meaning to "reliability"?

    A. Consistency B. Interpretability
    C. Objectivity D. Truthfulness

15. Which of the following can be classified as an observational device?

    A. Anecdotal records
    B. Interest inventories
    C. Projective technique
    D. Personality inventories

16. As a guidance counselor, you may often be consulted by parents about how to respond more helpfully to teenagers. Which one of the following judgments about parent-teenager relationships is false?

    A. Parents' approval of work well done and pride in accomplishment means a great deal to the teenager, even though he brushes it off.
    B. For the sake of the young person's self-respect, it is a good idea to criticize him as much as possible.
    C. Giving a teenager opportunity for being in with a group is closely related to school progress.
    D. Parents' recognition and appreciation of good school progress, without putting on heavy pressure, is a help in keeping it up

17. In counseling, the term "understanding" refers to

    A. the counselor's ability to communicate how a client's behavior appears to other people
    B. the counselor's skill in grasping meanings the client's comments convey
    C. the counselor's adeptness in anticipating feelings of the client
    D. the counselor's knowledge of dynamics of personality

18. Of the following, the MOST significant difference between "psychotherapy" and "counseling" is in the

    A. goals and expected outcomes
    B. techniques used
    C. amount of psychological insight involved
    D. professional background of the counselor

19. Appropriate "bridges" for the counselor in counseling are all of the following EXCEPT

    A. "Let's move on to..."
    B. "We were talking about..."
    C. "What was it you said about...?"
    D. "How does this fit in with what you said earlier?"

20. From the client-centered point of view, "understanding" in counseling is BEST thought of as

    A. diagnosing the client's motivational structure
    B. seeing the client's world as he sees it
    C. following and accepting the client's spoken words
    D. the ability to predict future actions

21. The statement of a client MOST indicative of *transference* feelings is:

    A. "I really didn't feel like coming here today."
    B. "My mother doesn't approve of my talking to you."
    C. "If only you would tell me what I should do."
    D. "You remind me of my father."

22. In counseling, "reflection" refers to

    A. a restatement of the counselee's comment
    B. clarification of the content of the remark
    C. the counselor's perception of the feelings being expressed
    D. a non-committal statement such as "uh huh"

23. In the given paradigm, all are CORRECTLY matched EXCEPT:

	Counseling Model	Predominant Goal
A.	Psychoanalytic	insight
B.	Teacher-learner	sound decision and self-understanding
C.	Behavioral	shaping of specific responses
D.	Client-centered	catharsis

24. Freud believes that the client builds defenses against his inner conflicts when the therapeutic process tempts him to express conflictual impulses. These defenses result in resistance.
According to Freud, such resistance in successful counseling

    A. is unavoidable
    B. is carefully avoided by the counselor
    C. indicates the counselor has proceeded too fast
    D. does not occur

25. Existential counseling includes all of the following characteristics EXCEPT

    A. a belief in universal values
    B. a subjective view of reality
    C. the total empathic response of the therapist
    D. the individual's intense awareness of his contingency and his freedom

KEY (CORRECT ANSWERS)

1.	C	11.	A
2.	A	12.	B
3.	B	13.	A
4.	A	14.	A
5.	D	15.	A
6.	D	16.	B
7.	D	17.	B
8.	D	18.	A
9.	B	19.	A
10.	C	20.	B
21.	D		
22.	C		
23.	D		
24.	A		
25.	A		

EXAMINATION SECTION
TEST 1

DIRECTIONS: Each question or incomplete statement is followed by several suggested answers or completions. Select the one that BEST answers the question or completes the statement. *PRINT THE LETTER OF THE CORRECT ANSWER IN THE SPACE AT THE RIGHT.*

1. Which one of the following "suggestions to interviewers" should be AVOIDED?

    A. Encourage the client to verbalize his thoughts and feelings.
    B. Cover as much as possible in each interview.
    C. Don't hesitate to refer the client to someone else who might be more helpful in the situation.
    D. The problem which is presented initially, or the one which seems most obvious, often is not the real one.

2. If it seems clear that disturbance in parents' marital relationships is a major factor in causing a child to be emotionally disturbed, the counselor should

    A. point this out to the parents and tell them that for the welfare of their children, they should resolve their difficulties
    B. suggest that he will be willing to discuss their marital difficulties with them
    C. ignore this and concentrate on helping the child
    D. tactfully suggest that their marital difficulties may be playing a part in their child's disturbance and offer to refer the parents to a qualified marriage counseling service

3. The process of collecting, analyzing, synthesizing and interpreting information about the client should be

    A. completed prior to counseling
    B. completed early in the counseling process
    C. limited to counseling which is primarily diagnostic in purpose
    D. continuous throughout counseling

4. Catharsis, the "emotional unloading" of the client's feelings, has a value in the early stages of counseling because it accomplishes all BUT which one of the following goals?

    A. It relieves strong physiological tensions in the client.
    B. It increases the client's anxiety and therefore his motivation to continue counseling.
    C. It provides a verbal substitute for "acting out" the client's aggressive feelings.
    D. It releases emotional energy which the client has been using to maintain his defenses.

5. During the first interview, the counselor can expect the client to participate at his BEST when the counselor

    A. structures the nature of the counseling process
    B. attempts to summarize the client's problem for him
    C. allows the client to verbalize at his own pace
    D. tells the client that he understands the presenting problem

6. To obtain the most effective results in change of attitude and behavior through parent education, the leader should be

   A. thoroughly grounded in the whole field of psychology
   B. able to help members of the group look at their own attitudes and behavior in constructive ways
   C. completely confident as to the right solution to problems that may be brought up
   D. a warm, charming, friendly human being

7. A social worker's report about a client states that a mother has ambivalent feelings concerning her child. This means that the mother

   A. has contradictory emotional reactions concerning her child
   B. is overprotective of the child
   C. strongly rejects the child
   D. is unduly apprehensive about the child's welfare

8. A psychological report notes, "The client shows little effect." This means that the client

   A. did not take the test too seriously
   B. did not show emotional behavior in situations which normally call for such reactions
   C. did not show signs of fatigue as the testing progressed
   D. reacted to the test situation in a generally favorable manner

9. A psychologist's report states, in part, that a client exhibits some masochistic symptoms. This will be evident to the counselor through the client's persistent attempts at

   A. self-assertion
   B. self-effacement
   C. inflicting physical harm on others
   D. sexual molestation of others of the same sex

10. According to research studies, the type of counselor response that is MOST often followed by a client's expression of insight or illumination is

    A. clarification of feeling
    B. reflection of feeling
    C. simple acceptance
    D. exploratory question

11. Of the following, the BEST way to deal with a 12-year-old boy who feels inferior to his peers is to

    A. provide tasks which he can master with little difficulty
    B. show him how irrational his feelings are
    C. accept his declarations of lack of confidence sympathetically
    D. carefully arrange situations in which he will be obliged to show leadership

12. In counseling or psychotherapy, the factor which is the MOST important for success tends to be the

    A. counselor's theoretical orientation
    B. counselor's attitudes and feelings toward the client

C. techniques used by the counselor
D. amount of experience and training possessed by the counselor

13. Transference is an important aspect of

    A. test construction
    B. grade placement
    C. anecdotal record keeping
    D. therapy

14. The MOST desirable way of establishing rapport with a client who comes to the counselor with a problem is to

    A. demonstrate sincere interest in him
    B. offer to do everything possible to solve his problem for him
    C. use the language of the client
    D. promise to keep his problem confidential

15. Role playing has been used as a technique in parent education work. Of the following, the major value is that it

    A. permits parents to express unconscious feelings and thereby solve conflicts
    B. tells a story in a forceful and therefore lasting way
    C. provides an opportunity for the individual to view his problems by standing off and looking at them through the eyes of someone else
    D. brings to light problems people never knew they had

16. If during a counseling situation a client expressed anger about a particular situation, which of the following responses would a non-directive counselor MOST likely make?

    A. "Why are you so angry?"
    B. "Is there any need to get so upset about this?"
    C. "This has really made you very mad, hasn't it?"
    D. "Do you feel better now that you have expressed your anger?"

17. In a counseling process, the counselor should usually give information

    A. whenever it is needed
    B. at the end of the process
    C. in the introductory interview
    D. just before the client would ordinarily request it

18. "After having recognized and clarified feelings and conflicts, it is usually necessary to go beyond the stage of understanding and to elaborate a constructive plan for future action." Which of the following people would NOT go along with the above statement?

    A. Thorne
    B. Robinson
    C. Williamson
    D. Rogers

19. The counselor should focus his attention in the beginning upon

    A. the transference phenomenon
    B. evidences of hostility
    C. the unique characteristics of the particular relationship at hand
    D. indications of client aggressiveness

20. A recent guidance text that stresses the broad developments of our national heritage, our contemporary social setting, our value patterns, and also the integration into guidance of many disciplines-sociology, anthropology, philosophy, psychology-is

   A. FOUNDATIONS OF GUIDANCE - Miller
   B. GUIDANCE POLICY AND PRACTICE - Mathewson
   C. GUIDANCE IN TODAY'S SCHOOLS - Mortenson & Schmuller
   D. GUIDANCE SERVICES - Humphreys, Traxler & North

21. Which one of the following characteristics of counseling is inconsistent with the others?

   A. Counseling is more than advice-giving.
   B. Counseling involves something more than the solution to an immediate problem.
   C. Counseling concerns itself with attitudes rather than actions.
   D. Counseling involves intellectual rather than emotional attitudes as its basic raw material.

22. One approach to counseling has been labeled "non-directive". The word "non-directive" derives from the fact that, in this approach to counseling, the counselor

   A. does not tell the client what he should do
   B. makes the client responsible for the direction of the course of the interviews
   C. does not make judgments about the behavior of the client
   D. avoids possible areas of threat to the client

23. Of the following personality traits, which would be LEAST essential for an effective counselor to possess?

   A. Extroversion   B. Objectivity
   C. Security   D. Sensitivity

24. Interpretation as a therapeutic tool is considered a hindrance to therapy progress by

   A. orthodox Freudians   B. neo-analysts
   C. Rogerians   D. Adlerians

25. The current interpersonal behavior of the client is probably MOST important as a therapy topic to which two analytic theorists?

   A. Freud and Adler   B. Adler and Rank
   C. Freud and Rank   D. Horney and Sullivan

KEY (CORRECT ANSWERS)

1.	B	11.	A
2.	D	12.	B
3.	D	13.	D
4.	B	14.	A
5.	C	15.	C
6.	B	16.	C
7.	A	17.	A
8.	B	18.	D
9.	B	19.	C
10.	C	20.	A

21. D
22. B
23. A
24. C
25. D

TEST 2

DIRECTIONS: Each question or incomplete statement is followed by several suggested answers or completions. Select the one that BEST answers the question or completes the statement. *PRINT THE LETTER OF THE CORRECT ANSWER IN THE SPACE AT THE RIGHT.*

1. When a counselor is listening to a client, it is MOST important that he be able to

    A. show interest and agreement with what the client is saying
    B. paraphrase what the client is saying
    C. understand the significance of what the client is saying
    D. differentiate between fact and fiction in what the client is saying

2. On which one of the following is successful counseling LEAST likely to depend?

    A. The counselor's theoretical orientation
    B. The counselor's ability to bring the client's feelings and attitudes into the open
    C. The counselor's diagnostic ability
    D. The client's readiness for counseling

3. A client is referred to you for counseling against his will and is suspicious and uncooperative. You should

    A. explain to him that you cannot help him unless he is prepared to cooperate
    B. explain that you are not taking sides and that you will be impartial
    C. show him that you know how he feels and encourage him to talk about it
    D. explain that you are on his side and will listen sympathetically to anything that he might care to bring up

4. Which one of the following would NOT be considered a basic objective of the first interview between a client and a counselor?

    A. Beginning a sound counseling relationship
    B. Identifying the client's real problem
    C. Opening up the area of client feelings and attitudes
    D. Clarifying the nature of the counseling process for the client

5. All of the following counselor statements or actions are appropriate techniques for ending an interview EXCEPT

    A. "Our time is nearly up. Is there something else you have in mind for today?"
    B. "Let's see now. Suppose we go over what we've accomplished today."
    C. Counselor may glance at his watch and say, "When would you like to come in again?"
    D. Counselor may shuffle papers on desk and say, "Now, let's see; when is my next appointment?"

6. It has been recognized in recent literature that the value structure of the individual counselor has what kind of effect on the counseling process?

    A. Direct
    B. Indirect
    C. Little
    D. None

7. The intensive study of the same individuals over a fairly long period of time represents the
   A. cross-sectional approach
   B. longitudinal approach
   C. clinical approach
   D. biographical approach

8. Of the following techniques, the one which is MOST characteristic of non-directive or client-centered therapy is
   A. encouraging transference
   B. free association
   C. reflection of feeling
   D. permissive questioning

9. In making predictions about how a client will behave in a given situation, a counselor
   A. should limit himself to those situations for which "actuarial" data are available
   B. must rely on "clinical" judgment in many situations but use "actuarial" data wherever possible
   C. should rely on "clinical" judgment in all situations, since they are more valid than "actuarial" predictions
   D. always uses "actuarial" data, but modifies them in light of his "clinical" impression of the client

10. A research study that establishes an hypothesis, sets up control groups, collects data, and generalizes from the data is
    A. formulative
    B. diagnostic
    C. experimental
    D. exploratory

11. The MOST usable single index of the social and economic status of all the members of any family is
    A. occupation of the father
    B. religious affiliation of the family
    C. location of the home in the community
    D. socio-economic rating by neighbors

12. When a counselor does NOT understand the meaning of a response that a counselee has made, the counselor usually should
    A. proceed to another topic
    B. admit his lack of understanding and ask for clarification
    C. act as if he understands so that the counselee's confidence in him is not shaken
    D. ask the counselee to choose his words more carefully

13. When the counselor makes a response which touches off a high degree of resistance in the counselee, he should
    A. apologize and rephrase his remark in a less threatening manner
    B. accept the resistance
    C. ignore the counselee's resistance
    D. recognize that little more will be accomplished in the interview and offer another appointment

14. Directive and non-directive counseling are two emphases in counseling theory and practice. From the pairs of names listed below, indicate the two that are representative of the Directive school.

    A. Thorne and Williamson
    B. Rogers and Thorne
    C. Williamson and Sullivan
    D. Sullivan and Rogers

15. Rogerian counseling theory is based on the assumption that the potential and tendency for growth toward a fully functioning personality is present in

    A. a few "self-actualized" persons
    B. most people of above average intelligence
    C. people whose behavior can be considered as "normal" and socially effective
    D. all people

16. Anecdotal records should contain which type(s) of information?

    A. Evaluations
    B. Interpretations
    C. Factual reports
    D. Prognoses

17. RESISTANCE in relation to psychological counseling typically refers to the

    A. client's defenses against his inner conflicts
    B. counselor's unwillingness to deal with the client's emotional problems
    C. client's having enough ego strength so that he can face his problems
    D. counselor's having enough ego strength so that he can help the client face his problems

18. On which one of the following does the democratic leader specifically rely? His ability to

    A. listen and tactfully guide the discussion in the direction he has planned and the members' willingness to cooperate
    B. diagnose situations, to interpret and explain them to the members and their willingness to accept
    C. discern the issues which the members could profitably discuss and his willingness to allow them with his help to do so
    D. understand the meaning of the response from the member's frame of reference and his willingness for them to make decisions

19. Advisement in counseling is MOST effective when the counselee is in a state of

    A. perceiving his problem as related to a conflict with inner forces
    B. minimal conflict and of optimal readiness for action
    C. perceiving his problem as related to an external conflict
    D. feeling extremely ambivalent about his self-concept

20. Of the following, the MOST valid use of projective techniques is the study of the

    A. problems which an individual faces
    B. cultural effects upon an individual
    C. inner world of an individual
    D. human relationships of an individual

21. Diagnosis is NOT regarded as a helpful antecedent to counseling by 21.____

    A. Cottle   B. Rogers
    C. Thorne   D. Williamson

22. The beginning counselor must be alert to interferences to rapport. Which one of the following is NOT considered an intereference? 22.____

    A. Injecting the counselor's present mood
    B. Engaging in "small talk" at the start of the interview
    C. Registering surprise or dismay
    D. Emphasizing the counselor's ability

23. There is some evidence according to Rogers that counseling is more effective with 23.____

    A. younger adults or higher intelligence
    B. older adults of higher intelligence
    C. younger adults of lower intelligence
    D. older adults of lower intelligence

24. In assisting with the scheduling of interviews for educational planning, the counselor should suggest that group instruction 24.____

    A. follow the counseling interview
    B. is not necessary when individual interviews can be scheduled since each case is different
    C. precede the counseling
    D. may either precede or follow the counseling interview

25. A client has requested an interview with the counselor to discuss a personal problem. In general, the BEST way to begin the interview is to 25.____

    A. come directly to the point and encourage the client to talk about his problem
    B. assure him that everything discussed will be confidential
    C. offer to help him in every way possible
    D. inquire whether he has discussed the problem with anyone else

KEY (CORRECT ANSWERS)

1.	C	11.	A
2.	A	12.	B
3.	C	13.	B
4.	B	14.	A
5.	D	15.	D
6.	A	16.	C
7.	B	17.	A
8.	C	18.	C
9.	B	19.	B
10.	C	20.	C
21.	B		
22.	B		
23.	A		
24.	C		
25.	A		

EXAMINATION SECTION
TEST 1

DIRECTIONS: Each question or incomplete statement is followed by several suggested answers or completions. Select the one that BEST answers the question or completes the statement. *PRINT THE LETTER OF THE CORRECT ANSWER IN THE SPACE AT THE RIGHT.*

1. The individual who emerges as the leader of a group is *usually*

   A. the person who, in the judgment of the group, can best meet the demands of the particular problem
   B. superior to the other members of the group in a wide variety of abilities
   C. chosen on the basis of personal qualities rather than ability
   D. the same person, no matter in what activities the group participates

   1.____

2. The status of an individual in a group is determined, *for the most part,* by

   A. the possession of those qualities the group deems important
   B. his socio-economic level
   C. his status in other groups of which he is a member
   D. the amount of time and energy he is willing to devote to the purposes of the group

   2.____

3. Among the following, the LEAST valid goal for the group discussion leader during the *first* sessions with the group is

   A. realization by the group of the distinction between an individual and his unacceptable behavior
   B. encouragement of self-revelation
   C. freedom to express any ideas or feelings for consideration by the group
   D. establishment of goals of mutual helpfulness

   3.____

4. Among the following, the LEAST valid way for the counselor to encourage a sense of acceptance on the part of everyone in the group is to

   A. be nonjudgmental with respect to all contributions from the group
   B. use the technique of reflection to help clarify statements
   C. give advice when the need is apparent
   D. call attention to existing limits when necessary

   4.____

5. The MOST distinctive characteristic of group counseling with younger children is the

   A. use of objects and play
   B. setting of the group
   C. lack of verbal communication
   D. non-directive role of the counselor

   5.____

6. Recent studies of individuals working in groups and individuals working alone have shown that

   A. elementary school clients work better alone; junior high school clients work better in groups
   B. the quality of work completed by a given individual is much the same whether he works alone or as a member of a group

   6.____

C. larger groups do better work than smaller groups working on similar tasks
D. individuals working in groups will show a high level of performance only when a group goal serves as a motivating force

7. New standards are MOST readily accepted by the members of groups when those members

   A. share in developing and establishing the standards
   B. personally know the leader who advocates the standards
   C. belong to an in-group which advocates the standards
   D. appreciate the weaknesses of the older standards

8. Group counseling differs from group therapy in that transference

   A. is interpreted in group counseling and not in group therapy
   B. is non-existent in group counseling
   C. is understood in group counseling but not interpreted
   D. reactions are discouraged in group therapy

9. Which one of the following objectives BEST describes the goal of group counseling?

   A. Broadening occupational horizons
   B. Use of peer group pressure
   C. Attitude change
   D. Helping larger numbers of people

10. In group counseling, the MOST effective communication results when the counselor-leader

    A. attempts to maintain one-way communication with individual group members
    B. becomes a member of the group and encourages two-way communication among all the members of the group including himself
    C. maintains two-way communication with individual clients and also permits some communication among clients on a rather formal basis
    D. tries to develop two-way communication with individual clients

11. "Group Dynamics" means a variety of things to many people. Which of the following is the soundest concept of the term?

    A. The structure of the group
    B. The techniques used in the group situation
    C. The factors making for productivity or failure
    D. The forces operating in the group situation

12. A group project should be defined as "multiple counseling" only if

    A. more than two group members achieve therapeutic relationships with the counselor
    B. there is a leader-participant relationship in group meetings
    C. it improves skills in human relationships
    D. individual counseling accompanies the group activity

13. Group counseling as a technique is MOST similar to which one of the following? 13.____

    A. Group guidance B. Socio-drama
    C. Social group work D. Group therapy

14. Of the following, what kind of behavior is usually manifested by the group working with a counselor in the first stages of small group sessions? 14.____

    A. Blocking B. Externalizing
    C. Rejecting D. Accepting

15. Role playing can be used effectively in group dynamics when 15.____

    A. real acting ability is present
    B. the player identifies spontaneously in feeling or attitude with real or imagined persons
    C. situations to be dramatized are carefully planned, structured and resolved
    D. there are no conflicts in behavior or differences of opinion

16. In grouping maladjusted individuals for group counseling, the MOST important criterion, of the following, is homogeneity of 16.____

    A. intelligence B. social maturity
    C. personality deviations D. age

17. Of the following, the area of guidance which lends itself LEAST readily to group study and discussion is 17.____

    A. educational and vocational opportunities
    B. problems involving family relationships
    C. questions dealing with male-female relations
    D. problems involving deep-seated emotional disturbance

18. Which one of the following "suggestions to group leaders" should be AVOIDED? 18.____

    A. Prepare a "hidden agenda" for the group session and make sure it is executed.
    B. Allow minority views to be expressed.
    C. Help all group members to grow through contributing their best services to the group.
    D. Encourage individual group members to experiment with enacting the leader role.

19. Although therapists differ in their ideas about the ideal composition for a therapeutic group, which one of the following characteristics would they agree they prefer to EXCLUDE from their groups? 19.____

    A. Silent people B. Compliant individuals
    C. Chronic monopolists D. Noisy people

20. Upon entering a classroom during group guidance period, you find the clients spontaneously acting out a home situation involving a quarrel over going to the movies. You may MOST reasonably conclude that they are 20.____

    A. using the socio-drama to work out an understanding of their home relationships
    B. spending the time in free activity for the development of social attitudes
    C. performing a psychodrama for the solution of their personal problems
    D. preparing a play to be performed in the institution's auditorium

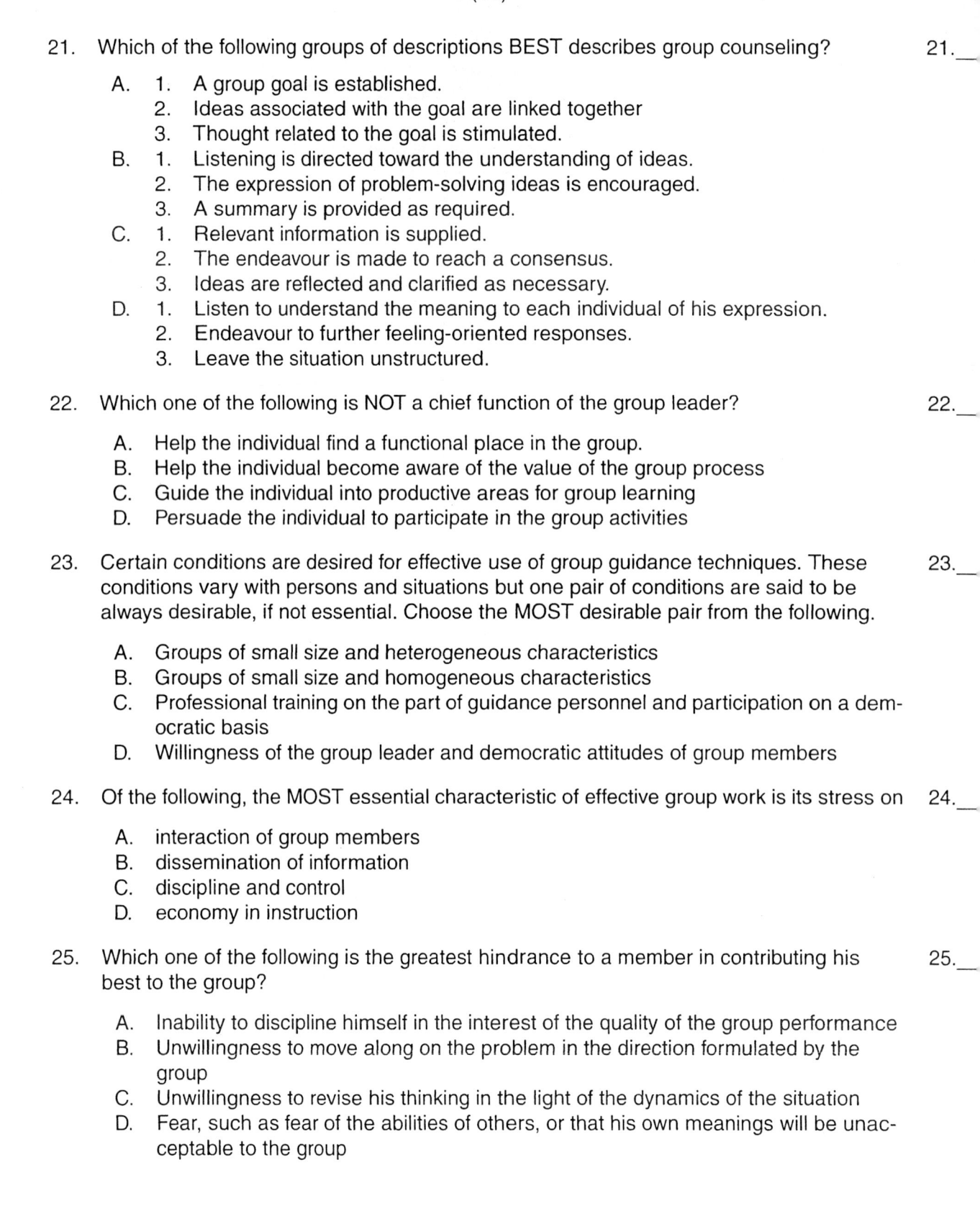

21. Which of the following groups of descriptions BEST describes group counseling?

    A. 1. A group goal is established.
        2. Ideas associated with the goal are linked together
        3. Thought related to the goal is stimulated.
    B. 1. Listening is directed toward the understanding of ideas.
        2. The expression of problem-solving ideas is encouraged.
        3. A summary is provided as required.
    C. 1. Relevant information is supplied.
        2. The endeavour is made to reach a consensus.
        3. Ideas are reflected and clarified as necessary.
    D. 1. Listen to understand the meaning to each individual of his expression.
        2. Endeavour to further feeling-oriented responses.
        3. Leave the situation unstructured.

22. Which one of the following is NOT a chief function of the group leader?

    A. Help the individual find a functional place in the group.
    B. Help the individual become aware of the value of the group process
    C. Guide the individual into productive areas for group learning
    D. Persuade the individual to participate in the group activities

23. Certain conditions are desired for effective use of group guidance techniques. These conditions vary with persons and situations but one pair of conditions are said to be always desirable, if not essential. Choose the MOST desirable pair from the following.

    A. Groups of small size and heterogeneous characteristics
    B. Groups of small size and homogeneous characteristics
    C. Professional training on the part of guidance personnel and participation on a democratic basis
    D. Willingness of the group leader and democratic attitudes of group members

24. Of the following, the MOST essential characteristic of effective group work is its stress on

    A. interaction of group members
    B. dissemination of information
    C. discipline and control
    D. economy in instruction

25. Which one of the following is the greatest hindrance to a member in contributing his best to the group?

    A. Inability to discipline himself in the interest of the quality of the group performance
    B. Unwillingness to move along on the problem in the direction formulated by the group
    C. Unwillingness to revise his thinking in the light of the dynamics of the situation
    D. Fear, such as fear of the abilities of others, or that his own meanings will be unacceptable to the group

KEY (CORRECT ANSWERS)

1. A
2. A
3. B
4. C
5. A

6. D
7. A
8. C
9. C
10. B

11. D
12. D
13. D
14. B
15. B

16. B
17. D
18. A
19. C
20. A

21. D
22. D
23. C
24. A
25. D

TEST 2

DIRECTIONS: Each question or incomplete statement is followed by several suggested answers or completions. Select the one that BEST answers the question or completes the statement. *PRINT THE LETTER OF THE CORRECT ANSWER IN THE SPACE AT THE RIGHT.*

1. Of the following, the particular value of group guidance lies in the fact that

   A. topics which can be discussed in individual guidance can be discussed more economically in group guidance
   B. group guidance can be conducted by therapists
   C. it is easier to detect children who are emotionally disturbed in group guidance
   D. the group helps children express themselves more freely about common problems

2. Which statement is LEAST true with respect to group-centered counseling?

   A. Group-centered counseling is focused upon personality integration and growth rather than solution of particular problems.
   B. The emphasis is upon the emotional rather than the intellectual aspects of understanding.
   C. The counselor promotes insight directly, using interpretations and recommendations where necessary.
   D. The counselor encourages free expression by recognizing and accepting all expressions without displaying approval or disapproval.

3. In applying the findings of group dynamics to classroom management and learning, which of the following is NOT appropriate?

   A. Create an atmosphere with minimal anxiety and threat.
   B. Clients should be permitted to make the group decisions without the possibility of the therapist's overriding the decisions.
   C. Encourage free discussion and questioning in the classroom.
   D. Lecture methods are less effective devices for obtaining behavioral change than discussion methods.

4. In parent group education discussions, the role of the leader will LEAST likely be to

   A. set the framework for discussion from the members' own experiences
   B. get every member to talk
   C. elicit as many different experiences as possible on any one point in the discussion
   D. help the group move toward its own independent thinking

5. Of the following, the most significant goal in parent group education is to help

   A. isolated parents to socialize
   B. parents better understand their children's needs at different stages of development
   C. parents learn the best techniques for handling children
   D. parents ventilate their guilt feelings

6. In group guidance, the counselor would deal primarily with which of the following needs of students?

   A. Informational and attitudinal
   B. Therapeutic
   C. Informational and therapeutic
   D. Attitudinal and therapeutic

7. When a client in a group guidance session embarks upon a long discourse which is apparently tangential to the main topic under discussion, the leader should

   A. by a gentle reminder bring him back to the main topic before the group censures him
   B. without impatience await reactions from the group
   C. ask another group member if he understands the speaker's message
   D. ask the speaker if he would like to explain to the group his reason for this recountal

8. When a client opens group discussion by voicing extreme hostility against adults, the leader should

   A. interpret his remarks as a frequent reaction of youth
   B. present the adult point of view so there will be a complete picture for reference in further discussion
   C. indicate little interest in his remarks and initiate a more constructive theme
   D. encourage the group to develop the subject

9. Which of the following statements LEAST characterizes the professional parent education discussion group programs?

   A. They represent one of many parent education services.
   B. They draw from many different professional disciplines.
   C. They illustrate one type of group method, specifically defined as to goal, method and organizational structure.
   D. They serve to resolve inner emotional conflicts which parents may have.

10. If the findings of research in group dynamics are applicable to the classroom situation, one would expect clients enrolled in classrooms characterized by a "laissez-faire" approach to find it MOST difficult to

    A. work out plans in advance
    B. evaluate their own progress
    C. attack a new task
    D. make friends

11. The findings of research studies that have contrasted leaders and nonleaders in the same group generally agree that leaders are superior to nonleaders in

    A. intelligence
    B. ability to accept criticism
    C. ability to differentiate right from wrong
    D. intensity of interests

12. Research in group processes has demonstrated that an individual will accept the attitudes of a group if he

    A. is ambitious
    B. rebels against authority
    C. makes friends quickly
    D. is a passive drifter

13. In a group guidance lesson, airing prejudices and counter-prejudices will

    A. promote a willingness on the part of the clients to probe more deeply into the topic
    B. arouse antagonisms that might well have been allowed to be dormant
    C. serve to confuse the pupil by exposing him to conflicting opinions
    D. lead to constructive action by forcing the client to make a choice

14. As contrasted with the class in which activities are group controlled, the class dominated by the therapist

    A. provides little opportunity for social learning
    B. shows less mastery of course material
    C. increases client anxiety and frustration
    D. promotes self-understanding and self-direction

15. Excessive domination of a group of children by an adult leader tends to

    A. increase the cohesiveness of the members of the group
    B. suppress the initiative of the members of the group
    C. increase the awareness of the group members of group goals
    D. prevent the formation of subgroups and cliques

16. Studies of the characteristics of leaders have made it clear that the leader of a group

    A. contributes more to the satisfaction of the needs of the members of the group than any other member
    B. differs from the other members of the group in degree of acceptance of nongroup members
    C. is more concerned with his individual problems than other members of the group
    D. is willing to devote more time and energy to the purpose of the group than any other member

17. SOCIOMETRY IN GROUP RELATIONS was written by

    A. Truda T. Weil   B. Helen Jennings
    C. Frances Wilson   D. Helen Witmer

18. The ability of an individual to persist as the leader of a group depends upon the adaptability of the leader and the

    A. stability of the group structure
    B. size of the group
    C. sex of the group members
    D. socioeconomic level of the group members

19. Of the following, the one that is NOT a prerequisite for the spontaneous formation of a stable group from an aggregate of individuals is

    A. motivation in terms of a common objective
    B. communication among the individuals
    C. mutual acceptance among the prospective members of the group
    D. similarity in social class

20. The degree of cohesiveness that has been established in a group can be increased MOST effectively by

    A. increasing the amount of interaction in the group
    B. modifying the purposes for which the group has been organized
    C. increasing the size of the group
    D. having non-group members criticize the leadership of the group

21. Studies of small groups have indicated that the less cohesive the group, the

    A. less susceptible the group to disruption caused by loss of a leader
    B. more it realizes its lack of solidarity
    C. less strongly will it defend itself against external criticism
    D. less permissive will it be of deviations from group standards

22. After a group has formed and become a cohesive unit, psychologists have defined four additional stages in its development: (a) the group
    I. The group develops its own norms of behavior
    II. The group develops its own "atmosphere"
    III. The status and role of individuals in the group become differentiated.
    IV. Collective goals begin to emerge.
    The sequence in which these four stages generally appear is

    A. I, II, III, IV
    B. II, IV, III, I
    C. III, I, IV, II
    D. IV, III, I, II

23. Which one of the following traits is of most importance in enabling an individual to maintain long-term leadership of a group?

    A. Empathy
    B. Sympathy
    C. Selflessness
    D. Egotism

24. Of the following, group approaches are COMMONLY used for

    A. encounter, discussion, training, and administration
    B. education, counseling, therapy, and recreation
    C. counseling, recreation, catharsis, and crisis intervention
    D. counseling, leadership, administration, and training

25. The purposes of group counseling are the following, with the EXCEPTION of

    A. avoidance of treating pathology as such
    B. helping clients attain a better level of functioning
    C. modifying social and familial problems
    D. resolving intra-psychic conflicts

KEY (CORRECT ANSWERS)

1. D
2. C
3. B
4. B
5. B

6. A
7. B
8. D
9. D
10. C

11. A
12. C
13. A
14. A
15. B

16. A
17. B
18. A
19. D
20. A

21. C
22. D
23. A
24. B
25. D

EXAMINATION SECTION
TEST 1

DIRECTIONS: Each question or incomplete statement is followed by several suggested answers or completions. Select the one that BEST answers the question or completes the Statement. *PRINT THE LETTER OF THE CORRECT ANSWER IN THE SPACE AT THE RIGHT.*

1. Perhaps the GREATEST single element in the beginning stages of work with a group is the

    A. attainment of respect and almost "blind faith" on the part of the group
    B. worker's ability to accept the group "as it is"
    C. possession of a broad sense of humor
    D. ability to bring together members with similar problems and personality traits
    E. ability to raise enough money to support the group properly

    1.____

2. The ONLY way in which a group worker can determine the stage of development of the group is to

    A. study the behavior of each individual member of the group
    B. study the behavior responses of the group individually and collectively
    C. discontinue the "pre-group" stages temporarily and study the reaction
    D. ask each member individually what his feelings are on the subject
    E. consult the records of the group

    2.____

3. All groups at one time or another feel hostile toward their worker or agency, and such behavior is

    A. dangerous and must be suppressed at once
    B. best alleviated by ejecting the hostile protagonists from the group
    C. normal and should be handled as such
    D. usually a sign that the agency or worker is lacking in some way
    E. not helpful to the group or worker and, therefore, the best solution is to terminate the meetings until such feelings have subsided

    3.____

4. To a group worker, the writing of records and reports is

    A. not necessary but can be a useful aid to his job
    B. an important part of his responsibility
    C. unimportant compared to the more "human" aspects of his job
    D. an uninteresting and unexciting part of his job that must be done
    E. clinical and impersonal, and has no place in the area of true social work

    4.____

5. Of the following objectives of having children work in committees, the MOST important is to

    A. develop self-direction in the areas of the social amenities and of parliamentary procedure
    B. improve children's ability in speaking effectively before a group
    C. develop initiative and leadership qualities of the bright children and encourage the shy children

    5.____

D. make learning a cooperative enterprise in thinking through and solving problems
E. stimulate competition within and between groups which will serve to promote greater interest in the group activity

6. The one of the following which is a device to be used in group dynamics is
   A. metronoscope
   B. opaque projector
   C. diorama
   D. sociogram
   E. group profile

7. The findings of research studies that have contrasted leaders and non-leaders in the same group generally agree that leaders are superior to non-leaders in
   A. making adjustments to new situations
   B. ability to accept criticism
   C. intensity of interests
   D. ability to differentiate right from wrong
   E. intelligence

8. Research in group processes has demonstrated that an individual will accept the attitudes of a group if he
   A. is ambitious
   B. is a passive drifter
   C. makes friends quickly
   D. rebels against authority
   E. strongly desires group membership

9. Boys and girls are generally most inclined toward group experiences with members of their own sex when they are between
   A. 2 and 3 years of age
   B. 4 and 5 years of age
   C. 6 and 10 years of age
   D. 11 and 14 years of age
   E. 15 and 18 years of age

10. Of the following, the unique kind of assistance which group counseling provides for a socially maladjusted client is
    A. the opportunity for the client to identify with a stable adult
    B. the special type of social environment which the counseling group affords the client
    C. the client's growing conviction that he has been "chosen" for the group
    D. a lightened academic load to compensate for the time and energy used in the group
    E. the client's belief that he is a fully accepted member of this group

11. In grouping maladjusted clients for group counseling, the MOST important criterion, of the following, is homogeneity of
    A. intelligence
    B. social maturity
    C. personality deviations
    D. age
    E. sex

12. The acceptance of an individual by an already functioning group will depend MOST upon the   12.____

    A. degree of authoritative ability which the individual can demonstrate before the group
    B. contribution the individual can make to realization of the group's goals
    C. influence which the individual enjoys in the community as a whole
    D. ability of the individual to provoke the group to concerted action
    E. extent to which the individual accepts the group's norms of behavior

13. Which one of the following is NOT characteristic of the development of a group?   13.____

    A. Emergence of collective goals
    B. Solidification of individual roles within the group structure
    C. Growth of group norms for behavior
    D. Development of a group atmosphere of social climate
    E. Stability of leadership, membership, and group goals

14. "Group Dynamics" means a variety of things to many people. Which of the following is the soundest concept of the term?   14.____

    A. The structure of the group
    B. The techniques used in the group situation
    C. The factors making for productivity or failure
    D. The forces operating in the group situation
    E. The processes of response and adjustment

15. The status of an individual in a group is determined, for the most part, by   15.____

    A. the possession of those qualities the group deems important
    B. his socio-economic level
    C. his status in other groups of which he is a member
    D. the amount of time and energy he is willing to devote to the purposes of the group
    E. his superior ability in guiding the group in formulating, organizing, and realizing its goals

16. The leader of a group of 12-year-old girls is MOST likely to be superior to the other members of the group in   16.____

    A. ability to make friends
    B. appearance
    C. school work
    D. artistic or musical talent
    E. status in other groups to which they belong

17. Of the following, the single characteristic MOST important in determining an individual's status in a group of preadolescent boys is   17.____

    A. intelligence   B. physical ability
    C. school marks   D. language development
    E. personality

4 (#1)

18. Of the following, the MOST important condition underlying the formation of an out-of-school group of eleven-year-old girls is

    A. coming from the same socio-economic level
    B. showing the same signs of physical development
    C. having the same attitudes and interests
    D. being in the same grade at school
    E. having parents who are close friends and who encourage the formation of the group

18.___

19. Recent studies of the productivity of individuals while working as members of a group on a joint project have demonstrated that

    A. larger groups are more productive than smaller groups working on similar tasks
    B. individuals function in much the same way in groups as they do in solitary situations
    C. a group goal is needed to motivate individuals to higher levels of performance
    D. high school pupils work better in groups; college students, as individuals
    E. even when a group goal is sought, individuals will always continue to compete on a personal level

19.___

20. UNDERSTANDING GROUP BEHAVIOR OF BOYS AND GIRLS was written by

    A. Helen H. Jennings
    B. Ruth Cunningham
    C. Jane Waters
    D. Alice V. Crow
    E. Sheldon Glueck

20.___

21. In comparison with other members of a group, the leader tends to

    A. hold himself in higher esteem
    B. be less spontaneous
    C. be more desirous of being of service to others
    D. be more willing to accept a low level of performance from members of the group
    E. be more authoritative and less compassionate

21.___

22. The individual who emerges as the leader of a group is usually

    A. the person with the highest status but not necessarily the best abilities
    B. superior to the other members of the group in a wide variety of abilities
    C. chosen on the basis of personal qualities rather than ability
    D. the same person, no matter in what activities the group participates
    E. the person who, in the judgment of the group, can best meet the demands of the particular problem

22.___

23. The degree of cohesiveness which has been established in a group is MOST likely to be lowered by

    A. unfavorable evaluation of the group by outsiders
    B. favorable evaluation of the group by outsiders
    C. decreasing the amount of interaction in the group
    D. increasing the degree of interaction in the group
    E. altering the membership of the group but increasing the degree of interaction

23.___

24. Research has shown that neighborhood gangs tend to be more cohesive than groups of the same age functioning as clubs in more formal youth agencies. This would suggest that

   A. the club is potentially longer-lived than the gang
   B. young people join clubs only if they are not accepted by the gang
   C. clubs will not be able to function adequately in a given neighborhood until some way is found to destroy gangs already in existence
   D. the activities of the gang meet the needs of its members better than those of the club program do
   E. the clubs are dominated by adults, thus limiting the expressiveness of its members

24._____

25. Studies of the cohesiveness of small groups have indicated that the more cohesive a group, the

   A. less likely is it that the group will allow any alteration in its present membership
   B. less likely is it that the group will permit internal disagreement with its objective or goals
   C. less perceptive is the group of its own solidarity
   D. more susceptible is the group to disruption caused by loss of a leader
   E. more willing will the group be to defend itself against external criticism

25._____

KEY (CORRECT ANSWERS)

1. B
2. B
3. C
4. B
5. D

6. D
7. E
8. C
9. C
10. B

11. B
12. E
13. B
14. D
15. A

16. A
17. B
18. D
19. C
20. B

21. A
22. E
23. C
24. D
25. E

TEST 2

DIRECTIONS: Each question or incomplete statement is followed by several suggested answers or completions. Select the one that BEST answers the question or completes the statement. *PRINT THE LETTER OF THE CORRECT ANSWER IN THE SPACE AT THE RIGHT.*

1. Which one of the following statements does NOT describe a function of group prejudice?
   A. It provides a source of egotistic satisfaction.
   B. It justifies various types of discrimination which are considered to be advantageous to the dominant group.
   C. It provides an outlet for aggressive feelings.
   D. It provides convenient scapegoats.
   E. It excludes most of those who are patently "undesirables" from participation in community activities.

2. The essence of _____ groups is that they are personal, intimate, diffuse, spontaneous, and affective (permeated by emotion).
   A. tertiary
   B. secondary
   C. primary
   D. marital
   E. centenary

3. The practice of group psychotherapy basically utilizes the fact that
   A. people generally tend to prefer group discussion to individually working out a problem
   B. attitudes and other characteristics are often group-formed and group-influenced
   C. private treatment is beyond the income of the average man
   D. fears, hostilities, etc. can be acted out rather than spoken about
   E. it is based on practical life situations, i.e., employment, family problems, etc.

4. The ability of an individual to persist as the leader of a group depends upon the availability of the leader and the
   A. stability of the group structure
   B. socioeconomic level of the group members
   C. size of the group
   D. sex of the group members
   E. "productiveness" of his efforts

5. Of the following, the MOST important determinant of leadership in pre-adolescent children is the child's
   A. self-confidence
   B. sex
   C. physical attractiveness
   D. socio-economic status
   E. intelligence level

6. Research in group processes has demonstrated that an individual will accept the attitudes of a group if he
   A. is ambitious
   B. is a passive drifter
   C. makes friends quickly
   D. rebels against authority
   E. is a "follower" rather than a "leader"

7. As contrasted with the class in which activities are group controlled, the class dominated by the therapist

   A. provides little opportunity for social learning
   B. shows less mastery of course material
   C. increases client anxiety and frustration
   D. promotes self-understanding and self-direction
   E. discourages clients from developing relationships with their peers

7.____

8. Excessive domination of a group of children by an adult leader tends to

   A. prevent the formation of subgroups and cliques
   B. suppress the initiative of the members of the group
   C. increase the cohesiveness of the members of the group
   D. increase the awareness of the group members of group goals
   E. accelerate the rate at which group goals are realized

8.____

9. Of the following, the one that is NOT a prerequisite for the spontaneous formation of a stable group from an aggregate of individuals is

   A. motivation in terms of a common objective
   B. communication among the individuals
   C. mutual acceptance among the prospective members of the group
   D. similarity in social class
   E. common allegiance to a cause

9.____

10. The degree of cohesiveness that has been established in a group can be increased MOST effectively by

    A. increasing the amount of interaction in the group
    B. modifying the purposes for which the group has been organized
    C. increasing the size of the group
    D. having non-group members criticize the leadership of the group
    E. decreasing the size of the group but making it more heterogeneous

10.____

11. Studies of small groups have indicated that the less cohesive the group, the

    A. less permissive will it be of deviations from group standards
    B. less susceptible the group to disruptions caused by loss of a leader
    C. less strongly will it defend itself against external criticism
    D. more it realizes its lack of solidarity
    E. less willing it is to submit to an authoritarian leader

11.____

12. Studies of the characteristics of leaders have made it clear that the leader of a group

    A. contributes more to the satisfaction of the needs of the members of the group than any other member
    B. differs from the other members of the group in degree of acceptance of nongroup members
    C. is willing to devote more time and energy to the purpose of the group than any other member
    D. is more concerned with his individual problems than other members of the group
    E. is superior to any other group member in social maturity and mental ability

12.____

13. Most of the boys in the seventh grade participate informally in a neighborhood group which has many characteristics of a gang. Mark is clearly the leader, while Terry is his most influential lieutenant; Sig has probably the lowest status in the group while Wally, who lives in the neighborhood, seems to have no part in their activities and no interest in the gang. The boy most likely to change his personal views to coalesce with what he sees as the group norm is

    A. Mark
    B. Terry
    C. Sig
    D. Wally
    E. either Mark or Terry

14. In attempting to make use of the findings of group dynamics in classroom management and learning, which of the following procedures is NOT appropriate?

    A. Creating an atmosphere with minimal anxiety and threat field
    B. Permitting students to make the group's decisions without the possibility of the teacher's overruling these decisions
    C. Encouraging free discussion and questioning in the classroom
    D. Regarding lecture methods as less effective devices for obtaining behavioral changes than discussion methods
    E. Extending the fields of client-therapist planning

15. The MOST important factor conducive to successful group work

    A. is initiative and self-direction on the part of the client
    B. is effective classroom management on the part of the therapist
    C. requires that necessary materials be placed within easy reach of the clients
    D. requires that memoranda to show the sequence of activities to be followed by different groups be written on the blackboard
    E. is effective classroom management by a class-elected leader

16. If group work is to be effective,

    A. there must be more than three groups
    B. the children must receive training in responsibility for their own activities
    C. group duties should not be rotated for long periods of time
    D. the therapist should always select the groups
    E. the groups must be stable and homogeneous

17. In most cases, groups should

    A. be based on the abilities of the client
    B. be based on the interests, abilities and achievements of the client
    C. consist of the same clients for all curriculum areas
    D. be based primarily on the physical limitations of the children
    E. be based on the results of sociometric tests

18. After a group has formed and become a cohesive unit, psychologists have defined four additional stages in its development: 18.____
    I. The group develops its own norms of behavior
    II. The group develops it own "atmosphere"
    III. The status and role of individuals in the group become differentiated
    IV. Collective goals begin to emerge
    The sequence in which these four stages generally appear is

    A. III, I, IV, II   B. I, II, III, IV   C. II, IV, III, I
    D. III, IV, I, II   E. IV, III, I, II

19. In a group guidance lesson, airing prejudices and counter-prejudices will   19.____

    A. promote a willingness on the part of the clients to probe more deeply into the topic
    B. lead to constructive action by forcing the client to make a choice
    C. arouse antagonisms that might well have been allowed to be dormant
    D. serve to confuse the client by exposing him to conflicting opinions
    E. lead to hostile feelings between clients with opposing points of view

20. During the past twenty years, there has been considerable research to determine the effectiveness of communication nets in small groups. Two of the simplest of the nets are: 20.____

    In each of these, the letter represents an individual and the line a means of two-way communication. The findings, to date, have tended to support the view that the use of network I rather than network II will result in

    A. less enthusiasm among the participants
    B. slower action in solving problems
    C. higher morale in the group as a whole
    D. greater adaptability to change
    E. less flexibility in making administrative decisions

21. For group work to be MOST effective in the teaching of reading in a fourth grade class, the groups should consist of participants who are chosen in terms of their being similar in   21.____

    A. emotional age   B. intelligence quotient
    C. mental age   D. reading age
    E. chronological age

22. What phase of group therapy *usually* causes the most disequilibrium within the group?   22.____

    A. Getting acquainted stage
    B. Minor acting out phase
    C. Major acting out phase
    D. The stage when the group becomes a group
    E. Termination of the group stage

23. Which phase of group therapy is the stage when extreme deviates have been removed and productive activity resumes?

    A. Getting acquainted stage
    B. Minor acting out phase
    C. Crescendo-of-tension phase
    D. The stage when the group becomes a group
    E. Termination of the group stage

24. Which phase of group therapy is the stage of GREATEST equilibrium in which consensus is easily reached and socially deviant behavior is at a minimum?

    A. Getting acquainted stage
    B. Minor acting out phase
    C. Major acting out phase
    D. The stage when the participant becomes a group
    E. Termination of the group stage

25. What information for a situation analysis model approach to the study of psychotherapy groups is included in the area of "setting"? The

    A. nature of the institution and the characteristics of the clientele
    B. emerging interactional patterns among the group members
    C. nature of the conflict as related to the focal event
    D. physical location and intervening aspects of the room
    E. background information that seems significantly related to the focal point

---

KEY (CORRECT ANSWERS)

1.	E	11.	C
2.	C	12.	A
3.	B	13.	B
4.	A	14.	B
5.	A	15.	B
6.	C	16.	B
7.	A	17.	B
8.	B	18.	E
9.	D	19.	A
10.	A	20.	A

21. D
22. E
23. C
24. A
25. E

EXAMINATION SECTION
TEST 1

DIRECTIONS: Each question or incomplete statement is followed by several suggested answers or completions. Select the one that BEST answers the question or completes the statement. *PRINT THE LETTER OF THE CORRECT ANSWER IN THE SPACE AT THE RIGHT.*

1. Which of the following is NOT an inherent characteristic of addiction?

    A. Tolerance changes
    B. Dissolution of relationships
    C. Physiological dependence
    D. Loss of self-control

    1.____

2. Which type of factor in an individual's predisposition to addiction has the GREATEST potential to increase the risk of addiction after exposure to a substance?

    A. Genetic   B. Constitutional   C. Psychological   D. Sociocultural

    2.____

3. The enabling behavior MOST likely practiced by the addicted person's family members in the early stages of addiction are

    A. cooperation and collaboration
    B. protecting and shielding
    C. codependence and cohabitation
    D. control and guilt

    3.____

4. When making initial inquiries about an addicted person's drug or alcohol abuse patterns and history, which of the following is probably the LEAST reliable?

    A. Information provided by the subject's friends and relatives
    B. Information provided by the patient or subject
    C. Medical histories of subject's family members
    D. Subject's medical record

    4.____

5. Which of the following is NOT one of the physical factors influencing addiction?

    A. Heredity
    B. Brain chemistry
    C. Metabolism
    D. Race

    5.____

6. In a recovery treatment center, which of the following behaviors or characteristics gives the STRONGEST indication that a subject is still addicted?

    A. Feeling caged or jailed
    B. Mood swings
    C. Nervousness
    D. Depression

    6.____

7. Which of the following is NOT true of *leverages* used by members of an intervention team to induce an addicted person to voluntarily submit to treatment?
They should

    A. only be used as a last resort
    B. not be carried out if they will result in isolating the addicted person
    C. be agreed upon and supported by every member of the intervention team
    D. not be threatened unless they will definitely be implemented

    7.____

8. What percentage of untreated alcoholics will eventually experience seizures?

    A. 5-15%   B. 20-30%   C. 40-50%   D. 55-75%

9. Which of the following is a sign that an adolescent has entered the late stages of addiction?

    A. Impulsiveness   B. Decrease in attention span
    C. Chronic depression   D. Denial

10. The type of drug dependency requiring the longest treatment time is USUALLY caused by

    A. alcohol   B. amphetamines
    C. opiates or cocaine   D. hallucinogens

11. Which of the following is NOT one of the primary factors in the formula that results in addiction?

    A. Drug effect   B. Social constraints
    C. Predisposition for abuse   D. Enabling factors

12. Drugs sometimes used in detoxification and which occupy a person's opiate-receptor sites without creating an accompanying sense of euphoria or loss of consciousness are

    A. opioids   B. opiates
    C. agonists   D. placebos

13. The normalization process during the late recovery phase of treatment includes

    A. increasingly sobriety-centered lifestyle
    B. discussion of drug hunger
    C. personality growth
    D. stress reduction techniques

14. Which of the following unconscious defense mechanisms, used by an addicted person, is characterized by partial awareness of the severity of the addiction?

    A. Denial   B. Minimization
    C. Rationalization D. Isolation

15. The characteristic of an addicted person's recovery illustrated by the person's attempt to repair the relationships damaged by his/her addiction is

    A. fellowship   B. surrender
    C. admission   D. restitution

16. Which of the following is a sign that a drinker has entered the late stages of alcoholism?

    A. Progressive increase in drinking
    B. Broken promises to friends and family
    C. Personality changes
    D. Malnutrition

17. An alcoholic subject is said to have entered stage four of the withdrawal process if he or she experiences

    A. seizures
    B. delirium tremens
    C. vomiting
    D. hallucinations

18. Which of the following unconscious defense mechanisms, used by an addicted person, is characterized by an avoidance of feelings through focusing on logic?

    A. Rationalization
    B. Intellectualization
    C. Repression
    D. Projection

19. Measuring from the starting point of detoxification, what is typically the amount of time required for a recovering person to regain the level of health and well-being associated with his/her pre-addiction lifestyle?

    A. 6 months   B. 1 year   C. 18 months   D. 3 years

20. A characteristic that typically differentiates teenage alcoholism from adult alcoholism is that teenagers

    A. are more likely to explain that they drink to celebrate or be sociable
    B. have a more difficult time with recovery
    C. claim drinking as an escape from life's problems
    D. sustain less physiological damage

21. Which type of recovery treatment is reserved for the most advanced cases of addiction?

    A. Day treatment
    B. Residential treatment
    C. Inpatient hospitalization
    D. Partial hospitalization

22. The use of which opiate drug typically carries the LOWEST risk for dependency or abuse?

    A. Percodan   B. Methadone   C. Codeine   D. Demerol

23. What is the APPROXIMATE mortality rate for alcoholic patients who suffer from delirium tremens?

    A. Zero   B. 1-10%   C. 10-20%   D. 20-30%

24. Addiction is a process influenced primarily by each of the following EXCEPT

    A. factors relating to the individual user
    B. various social factors
    C. factors relating to specific physiological health concerns
    D. factors relating to the drug being used

25. Which of the following statements about alcoholism is NOT true?

    A. Children of alcoholics often learn alcoholic behavior from their parents.
    B. Divorce, loss of a job, death of a loved one, and other life traumas can cause alcoholism.
    C. Alcoholism is often a symptom of larger psychological problems.
    D. An alcoholic in the throes of the disease drinks to avoid self-destruction.

KEY (CORRECT ANSWERS)

1.	B		11.	B
2.	A		12.	C
3.	B		13.	C
4.	B		14.	B
5.	D		15.	D
6.	A		16.	D
7.	B		17.	B
8.	A		18.	B
9.	C		19.	C
10.	C		20.	A

21. C
22. C
23. C
24. C
25. D

TEST 2

DIRECTIONS: Each question or incomplete statement is followed by several suggested answers or completions. Select the one that BEST answers the question or completes the statement. *PRINT THE LETTER OF THE CORRECT ANSWER IN THE SPACE AT THE RIGHT.*

1. Age, peers, and status are examples of _____ factors in an individual's predisposition to addiction. 1._____

   A. genetic B. constitutional C. psychological D. sociocultural

2. How many days should an alcoholic subject's detoxification process typically last? 2._____

   A. 1-10 B. 10-20 C. 20-30 D. 30-40

3. Which of the following is NOT true of the confrontation that takes place between members of an intervention team and an addicted person? 3._____
It must

   A. be rehearsed by all team members together
   B. involve quick-thinking people who can formulate responses to unanticipated statements
   C. involve people from a variety of the addicted person's life experiences
   D. be rigidly planned and structured

4. What is the characteristic of an addicted person's recovery illustrated by the person's expression of willingness to accept the help of treatment staff in the recovery process? 4._____

   A. Surrender B. Acceptance C. Fellowship D. Restitution

5. In the early stages of an addicted or alcoholic person's recovery, the process of nutritional repair should include each of the following EXCEPT 5._____

   A. three good meals a day
   B. total elimination of caffeine intake
   C. three nutritious snacks a day
   D. increasing the amount of sugars in the diet

6. Which of the following stages in the progression to freedom from addiction is considered to be the final stage, at which recovery is complete? 6._____

   A. Spiritual well-being   B. Mental well-being
   C. Total abstinence   D. Physical well-being

7. The FIRST goal of recovery treatment is to remedy _____ damage to the addicted person. 7._____

   A. social B. psychological C. physical D. spiritual

8. Which of the following steps should be taken LAST by friends/family members who want to practice intervention in a person's addiction? 8._____

   A. Devising a treatment plan
   B. Confronting the addicted person
   C. Getting help for the person's family
   D. Asking others for help

9. Each of the following is a disadvantage associated with the use of sedatives during an alcoholic subject's withdrawal EXCEPT that it

   A. increases suspicion and paranoia
   B. conflicts with the *abstinence* goal of detoxification
   C. lengthens the detoxification period
   D. interferes with the subject's alertness and early participation in treatment

10. Which of the following symptoms does addiction MOST commonly share with other chronic, debilitating diseases?

    A. Central nervous system damage
    B. Seizures
    C. Denial
    D. Physiological damage

11. An addicted person who would require one of the more intense levels of recovery treatment and care would PROBABLY have

    A. minor withdrawal symptoms
    B. family members who attend Al-Anon
    C. already be resigned to treatment
    D. already attempted recovery at least once and failed

12. The enabling behavior MOST likely practiced by the addicted person's family members in the advanced stages of addiction is

    A. cooperation   B. protecting
    C. codependence   D. guilt

13. Which of the following is NOT a symptom associated with stage two in an alcoholic subject's withdrawal process?

    A. Rapid heartbeat   B. Hand tremors
    C. Insomnia   D. Seizures

14. During intervention, participants on the intervention team should avoid describing to the addicted person

    A. concerns for the addicted person's health
    B. observed examples of addiction-related incidents
    C. observed consequences of addiction-related incidents
    D. personal assessment of emotional damage inflicted upon the addicted person's relations

15. During recovery, a subject sometimes becomes dependent on a drug that has the same relative effects on the central nervous system as the drug for which the subject is being treated.
    This is known specifically as

    A. substitution   B. cross-addiction
    C. surrender   D. submission

16. During an intervention, which of the following types of statements should be offered to the addicted person by members of the intervention team?   16.____

    A. Generalized comments   B. Judgments
    C. Observations   D. Opinions

17. Past failures, emotional trauma, and personality defects are examples of _____ factors in an individual's predisposition to addiction.   17.____

    A. genetic   B. constitutional
    C. psychological   D. sociocultural

18. The normalization process during the restabilization phase of recovery treatment includes   18.____

    A. introducing external motivations for recovery
    B. personality restructuring
    C. personality growth
    D. stress reduction techniques

19. Which characteristic typically differs between female and male alcoholics?   19.____

    A. Age
    B. Rate of advancement through addictive stages
    C. Likelihood of concurrent addiction to prescription drugs
    D. Professional status

20. Each of the following is an important factor determining the overall effects of addiction on a family EXCEPT   20.____

    A. the type of substance used
    B. the sex of addicted parent
    C. existing feelings of nonaddicted family members toward the addicted
    D. where and when substances are used

21. The component of a comprehensive addiction treatment program that is included in the category of psychosocial rehabilitation is   21.____

    A. social assessment   B. treating medical problems
    C. random drug screenings   D. detoxification

22. Each of the following is considered a warning sign for the onset of alcoholism's early stages EXCEPT   22.____

    A. alcohol-related problems B. hiding bottles
    C. changes in drinking patterns   D. preoccupation with alcohol

23. If sedatives are to be used by a subject during the alcoholic withdrawal period, APPROXIMATELY how long is the recommended period for their use?   23.____

    A. For the first overnight period
    B. For the first three or four days
    C. Until the subject does not appear to require sedation
    D. Throughout the entire period of detoxification

24. Which of the following is NOT one of the psychological factors influencing addiction? 24.___

    A. Coping mechanisms B. Denial
    C. Tolerance changes D. Reinforcing factors

25. The characteristic of an addicted person's recovery illustrated by the person's acknowledgement of his/her individual responsibility for recovery is termed 25.___

    A. surrender B. acceptance
    C. fellowship D. admission

KEY (CORRECT ANSWERS)

1.	D	11.	D
2.	A	12.	C
3.	B	13.	D
4.	A	14.	D
5.	D	15.	B
6.	A	16.	C
7.	C	17.	C
8.	B	18.	D
9.	A	19.	C
10.	C	20.	A

21. C
22. B
23. B
24. C
25. B

EXAMINATION SECTION
TEST 1

DIRECTIONS: Each question or incomplete statement is followed by several suggested answers or completions. Select the one that BEST answers the question or completes the statement. PRINT THE LETTER OF THE CORRECT ANSWER IN THE SPACE AT THE RIGHT.

1. When a counselor is planning a future interview with a client, of the following, the MOST important consideration is the

    A. recommendations he will make to the client
    B. place where the client will be interviewed
    C. purpose for which the client will be interviewed
    D. personality of the client

    1.____

2. For a counselor to make a practice of reviewing the client's case record, if available, prior to the interview, is, usually,

    A. *inadvisable,* because knowledge of the client's past record will tend to influence the counselor's judgment
    B. *advisable,* because knowledge of the client's background will help the counselor to identify discrepancies in the client's responses
    C. *inadvisable,* because such review is time-consuming and of questionable value
    D. *advisable,* because knowledge of the client's background will help the counselor to understand the client's situation

    2.____

3. Assume that a counselor makes a practice of constantly reassuring clients with serious and complex problems by making such statements as: "I'm sure you'll soon be well;" "I know you'll get a job soon;" or "Everything will be all right."
Of the following, the MOST likely result of such a practice is to

    A. encourage the client and make him feel that the counselor understands what the client is going through
    B. make the client doubtful about the counselor's understanding of his difficulties and the counselor's ability to help
    C. confuse the client and cause him to hesitate to take any action on his own initiative
    D. help the client to be more realistic about his situation and the probability that it will improve

    3.____

4. In order to get the maximum amount of information from a client during an interview, of the following, it is MOST important for the counselor to communicate to the client the feeling that the counselor is

    A. interested in the client
    B. a figure of authority
    C. efficient in his work habits
    D. sympathetic to the client's lifestyle

    4.____

5. Of the following, the counselor who takes extremely detailed notes during an interview with a client is *most likely* to

    A. encourage the client to talk freely

    5.____

B. distract and antagonize the client
C. help the client feel at ease
D. understand the client's feelings

6. As a counselor, you find that many of the clients you interview are verbally abusive and unusually hostile to you.
   Of the following, the MOST appropriate action for you to take *first* is to

   A. review your interviewing techniques and consider whether you may be provoking these clients
   B. act in a more authoritative manner when interviewing troublesome clients
   C. tell these clients that you will not process their applications unless their troublesome behavior ceases
   D. disregard the clients' troublesome behavior during the interview

7. During an interview, you did not completely understand several of your client's responses. In each instance, you rephrased the client's statement and asked the client if that was what he meant.
   For you to use such a technique during interviews would be considered

   A. *inappropriate;* you may have distorted the client's meaning by rephrasing his statements
   B. *inappropriate;* you should have asked the same questioE until you received a comprehensible response
   C. *appropriate;* the client will have a chance to correct you if you have misinterpreted his responses
   D. *appropriate;* a counselor should rephrase clients' responses for the records

8. A counselor is interviewing a client who has just had a severe emotional shock because of an assault on her by a mugger.
   Of the following, the approach which would generally be MOST helpful to the client is for the counselor to

   A. comfort the client and encourage her to talk about the assault
   B. sympathize with the client but refuse to discuss the assault with her
   C. tell the client to control her emotions and think positively about the future
   D. proceed with the interview in an impersonal and unemotional manner

9. A counselor finds that her questions are misinterpreted by many of the clients she interviews.
   Of the following, the MOST likely reason for this problem is that the

   A. client is not listening attentively
   B. client wants to avoid the subject being discussed
   C. counselor has failed to express her meaning clearly
   D. counselor has failed to put the client at ease

10. For a counselor to look directly at the client and observe him during the interview is generally

    A. *inadvisable;* this will make the client nervous and uncomfortable
    B. *advisable;* the client will be more likely to refrain from lying
    C. *inadvisable;* the counselor will not be able to take notes for the case record
    D. *advisable;* this will encourage conversation and accelerate the progress of the interview

11. You are interviewing a client who is applying for social services for the first time. In order to encourage this client to freely give you the information needed for you to establish his eligibility, of the following, the BEST way to start the interview is by

    A. asking questions the client can easily answer
    B. conveying the impression that his responses to your questions will be checked
    C. asking two or three similar but important questions
    D. assuring the client that your sole responsibility is "getting the facts"

12. Counselors are encouraged to record significant information obtained from clients and services provided for clients. Of the following, the MOST important reason for this practice is that these case records will

    A. help to reduce the need for regular supervisory conferences
    B. indicate to counselors which clients are taking up the most time
    C. provide information which will help the agency to improve its services to clients
    D. make it easier to verify the complaints of clients

13. As a counselor you find that interviews can be completed in a shorter period of time if you ask questions which limit the client to a certain answer.
    For you to use such a technique would be considered

    A. *inappropriate*, because this type of question usually requires advance preparation
    B. *inappropriate*, because this type of question may inhibit the client from saying what he really means
    C. *appropriate*, because you know the areas into which the questions should be directed
    D. *appropriate*, because this type of question usually helps clients to express themselves clearly

14. Assume that, while you are interviewing an individual to obtain information, the individual pauses in the middle of an answer.
    The BEST of the following actions for you to take at this time is to

    A. correct any inaccuracies in what he has said
    B. remain silent until he continues
    C. explain your position on the matter being discussed
    D. explain that time is short and that he must complete his story quickly

15. You have been assigned to interview the mother of a five-year-old son in her home to get information useful in locating the child's absent father. During the interview, you notice many serious bruises on the child's arms and legs, which the mother explains are due to the child's clumsiness. Of the following, your BEST course of action is to

    A. accept the mother's explanation and concentrate on getting information which will help you to locate the father
    B. advise the mother to have the child examined for a medical condition that may be causing his clumsiness
    C. make a surprise visit to the mother later, to see if someone is beating the child
    D. complete your interview with the mother and report the case to your supervisor for investigation of possible child abuse

16. During an interview, the former landlord of an absent father offers to help you to locate the father if you will give the landlord confidential information you have on the financial situation of the father.
Of the following, you should

    A. immediately end the interview with the landlord
    B. urge the landlord to help you but explain that you are not permitted to give him confidential information
    C. freely give the landlord the confidential information he requests about the father
    D. give the landlord the information only if he promises to keep it confidential

17. You feel that your client, a released mental patient, is not adjusting well to living on his own in an apartment. To gather more information, you interview privately his next-door neighbor, who claims that the client is creating a "disturbance" and speaks of the client in an angry and insulting manner.
Of the following, the BEST action for you to take in this situation is to

    A. listen patiently to the neighbor to try to get the facts about your client's behavior
    B. inform the neighbor that he has no right to speak insultingly about a mentally ill person
    C. make an appointment to interview the neighbor some other time when he isn't so upset
    D. tell the neighbor that you were not aware of the client's behavior and that you will have the client moved

18. As a counselor, you are interviewing a client to determine his eligibility for a work program. Suddenly the client begins to shout that he is in no condition to work and that you are persecuting him for no reason.
Of the following, your BEST response to this client is to

    A. advise the client to stop shouting or you will call for the security guard
    B. wait until the client calms down, then order him to come back for another interview
    C. insist that you are not persecuting the client and that he must complete the interview
    D. wait until the client calms down, say that you understand how he feels, and try to continue the interview

19. You are interviewing a mother whose 17-year-old son has recently been returned home from a mental institution. Although she is willing to care for her son at home, she is frightened by his strange and sometimes violent behavior and does not know the best arrangement to make for his care.
Of the following, your MOST appropriate response to this mother's problem is to

    A. describe the supportive services and alternatives to home care which are available
    B. help her to accept her son's strange and violent behavior
    C. tell her that she will not be permitted to care for her son at home if she is frightened by his behavior
    D. convince her that she is not responsible for her son's mental condition

20. Assume that you are interviewing an elderly man who comes to the center several times a month to discuss topics with you which are not related to social services. You realize that the man is lonely and enjoys these conversations.
Of the following, it would be MOST appropriate to

    A. politely discourage the man from coming in to pass the time with you
    B. avoid speaking to this man the next time he comes into the center
    C. explore with the client his feelings about joining a senior citizens' center
    D. continue to hold these conversations with the man

21. A client you are interviewing tends to ramble on after each response that he gives, so that many clients are kept waiting.
In this situation, of the following, it would be MOST advisable to

    A. try to direct the interview, in order to obtain the necessary information
    B. reduce the number of questions asked so that you can shorten the interview
    C. arrange a second interview for the client so that you can give him more time
    D. tell the client that he is wasting everybody's time

22. A non-minority counselor is about to interview a minority client on public assistance for job placement when the client says: "What does your kind know about my problems? You've never had to survive out on these streets."
Of the following, the counselor's MOST appropriate response in this situation is to

    A. postpone the interview until a minority counselor is available to interview the client
    B. tell the client that he must cooperate with the counselor if he wants to continue receiving public assistance
    C. explain to the client the function of the counselor in this unit and the services he provides
    D. assure the client that you do not have to be a member of a minority group to understand the effects of poverty

23. When you are interviewing someone to obtain information, the BEST of the following reasons for you to repeat certain of his exact words is to

    A. *assure* him that appropriate action will be taken
    B. *encourage* him to elaborate on a point he has made
    C. *assure* him that you agree with his point of view
    D. *encourage* him to switch to another topic of discussion

24. fou are interviewing a young client who seriously under-estimates the amount of education and training he will require for a certain occupation.
For you to tell the client that you think he is mistaken would generally be considered

    A. *inadvisable,* because counselors should not express their opinions to clients
    B. *inadvisable,* because clients have the right to self-determination
    C. *advisable,* because clients should generally be alerted to their misconceptions
    D. *advisable,* because counselors should convince clients to adopt a proper life style

25. Of the following, the MOST appropriate manner for a counselor to assume during an interview with a patient is   25.____

    A. authoritarian   B. paternal
    C. casual   D. businesslike

KEY (CORRECT ANSWERS)

1.	C	11.	A
2.	D	12.	C
3.	B	13.	B
4.	A	14.	B
5.	B	15.	D
6.	A	16.	B
7.	C	17.	A
8.	A	18.	D
9.	C	19.	A
10.	D	20.	C

21. A
22. C
23. B
24. C
25. D

TEST 2

DIRECTIONS: Each question or incomplete statement is followed by several suggested answers or completions. Select the one that *BEST* answers the question or completes the statement. *PRINT THE LETTER OF THE CORRECT ANSWER IN THE SPACE AT THE RIGHT.*

1. You are interviewing a legally responsible absent father who refuses to make child support payments because he claims the mother physically abuses the child.
   Of the following, the *BEST* way for you to handle this situation is to tell the father that you

   A. will report his complaint about the mother, but he is still responsible for making child support payments
   B. suspect that he is complaining about the mother in order to avoid his own responsibility for making child support payments
   C. are concerned with his responsibility to make child support payments, not with the mother's abuse of the child
   D. can not determine his responsibility for making child support payments until his complaint about the mother is investigated

   1.____

2. You are interviewing an elderly woman who lives alone to determine her eligibility for homemaker service at public expense. Though obviously frail and in need of this service, the woman is not completely cooperative, and during the interview, is often silent for a considerable period of time.
   Of the following, the *BEST* way for you to deal with these periods of silence is to

   A. realize that she may be embarrassed to have to apply for homemaker service at public expense, and emphasize her right to this service
   B. postpone the interview and make an appointment with her for a later date, when she may be better able to cooperate
   C. explain to the woman that you have many clients to interview and need her cooperation to complete the interview quickly
   D. recognize that she is probably hiding something and begin to ask questions to draw her out

   2.____

3. During a conference with an adolescent boy at a juvenile detention center, you find out for the first time that he would prefer to be placed in foster care rather than return to his natural parents.
   To uncover the reasons why the boy dislikes his own home, of the following, it would be *MOST* advisable for you to

   A. ask the boy a number of short, simple questions about his feelings
   B. encourage the boy to talk freely and express his feelings as best he can
   C. interview the parents and find out why the boy doesn't want to live at home
   D. administer a battery of psychological tests in order to make an assessment of the boy's problems

   3.____

4. You are interviewing a mother who is applying for Aid to Families with Dependent Children because the husband has deserted the family. The mother becomes annoyed at having to answer your questions and tells you to leave her apartment.
   Which one of the following actions would be *most appropriate* to take *FIRST* in this situation?

   4.____

A. Return to the office and close the case for lack of cooperation
B. Tell the mother that you will get the information from her neighbors if she does not cooperate
C. Tell the mother that you must stay until you get answers to your questions
D. Explain to the mother the reasons for the interview and the consequences of Her failure to cooperate

5. A counselor counseling juvenile clients finds that, although he can tolerate most of their behavior, he becomes infuriated when they lie to him.
Of the following, the counselor can BEST deal with his anger at his clients' lying by

A. recognizing his feelings of anger and learning to control expression of these feelings to his clients
B. warning his clients that he cannot be responsible for his anger when a client lies to him
C. using will power to suppress his feelings of anger when a client lies to him
D. realizing that lying is a common trait of juveniles and not directed against him personally

6. During an interview, one of your clients, a former drug addict, has expressed an interest in attending a community counseling center and resuming his education.
In this case, the MOST appropriate action that you should take FIRST is to

A. determine whether this ambition is realistic for a former drug addict
B. send the client's application to a community counseling center which provides services to former addicts
C. ask the client whether he is really motivated or is just seeking your approval
D. encourage and assist the client to take this step, since his interest is a positive sign

7. You are interviewing a client who, during previous appointments, has not responded to your requests for information required to determine his continued eligibility for services. On this occasion, the client again offers an excuse which you feel is not acceptable.
For you to advise the client of the probable loss of services because of his lack of cooperation is

A. *inappropriate,* because the threat to withhold services will harm the relationship between counselor and client
B. *inappropriate,* because counselors should not reveal to clients that they do not believe their statements
C. *appropriate,* because social services are a reward given to cooperative clients
D. *appropriate,* beca,us.e the counselor should Inform clients of the consequences of their lack of cooperation

8. Assume that you are counselling an adolescent boy in a juvenile detention center who has been a ringleader in smuggling "pot" into the center.
During your regular interview with this boy, of the following, it would be *advisable* to

A. tell him you know that he has been involved in smuggling pot and that you are trying to understand the reasons for his misbehavior
B. ignore his pot smuggling in order to reassure him that you understand and accept him, even though you do not agree with his standards of behavior
C. warn him that you have reported his pot smuggling and that he will be punished for his misbehavior
D. show him that you disapprove of his pot smuggling, but assure him that you will not report him for his misbehavior

9. Your unit has received several complaints about a homeless elderly woman living outdoors in various locations in the area. To help determine the need for protective services for this woman, you interview several persons in the neighborhood who are familiar with her, but all are uncooperative or reluctant to give information.
Of the following, your BEST approach to these persons is to explain to them that

   A. you will take legal steps against them if they do not cooperate with you
   B. their cooperation may enable you to help this homeless woman
   C. you need their cooperation to remove this homeless woman from their neighborhood
   D. they will be responsible for any harm that comes to this homeless woman

10. Assume that you are interviewing a client regarding an adjustment in budget. The client begins to scream at you that she holds you responsible for the decrease in her allowance.
Of the following, which is the BEST way for you to handle this situation?

   A. Attempt to discuss the matter calmly with the client and explain her right to a hearing
   B. Urge the client to appeal and assure her of your support
   C. Tell the client that her disorderly behavior will be held against her
   D. Tell the client that the reduction is "due to red tape" and is not your fault

11. As a counselor assigned to a juvenile detention center, you are having a counselling interview with a recently admitted boy who is having serious problems in adjusting to confinement in the center. During the interview, the boy frequently interrupts to ask you personal questions. Of the following, the BEST way for you to deal with these questions is to

   A. tell him in a friendly way that your job is to discuss his problems, not yours
   B. try to understand how the questions relate to the boy's own problems and reply with discretion
   C. take no notice of the questions and continue with the interview
   D. try to win the boy's confidence by answering his questions in detail

12. A counselor is interviewing an elderly woman who hesitates to provide necessary information about her finances to determine whether she is eligible for supplementary assistance. She fears that this information will be reported to others and that her neighbors will find out that she is destitute and applying for "welfare." Of the following, the counselor's MOST appropriate response is to

   A. tell her that, if she hesitates to give this information, the agency will get it from other sources
   B. assure her that this information is kept strictly confidential and will not be given to unauthorized persons
   C. convince her that her application will be turned down unless she provides this information as soon as possible
   D. ask for the name and address of her nearest relative and obtain the information from that person

13. You are counseling a couple whose children have been placed in a foster home because of the couple's quarreling and child neglect. When you interview the wife by herself, she tells you that she knows the husband often "cheats" on her with other women, but she is too afraid of the husband's temper to tell him how much this hurts her.
    For you to immediately reveal to the husband the wife's unhappiness concerning his "cheating" is, generally,

    A. *good practice,* because it will help the husband to understand why his wife quarrels with him
    B. *poor practice,* because information received from the wife should not be given to the husband without her permission
    C. *good practice,* because the husband will direct his anger at you rather than at his wife
    D. poor *practice,* because the wife may have told you a false story about her husband in order to win your sympathy

14. A counselor is beginning a job placement interview with a tall, strongly built young man. As the man sits down, the counselor comments: "I know a big fellow like you wouldn't be interested in any clerical job."
    For the counselor to make such a comment is, generally,

    A. *appropriate,* because it creates an air of familiarity which may put the man at ease
    B. *inappropriate,* because the man may be sensitive about his physical size
    C. *appropriate,* because, the counselor is using his judgment to help speed up the interview
    D. *inappropriate,* because the man may feel he is being pressured into agreeing with the counselor

15. A counselor in a men's shelter is counseling a middle-aged client for alcoholism. During counseling, the" client confesses that, many years ago, he had often enjoyed sexually abusing his ten-year-old daughter. The counselor tells the client that he personally finds the client's behavior "morally disgusting."
    For the counselor to tell the client this is, generally,

    A. *acceptable counseling practice,* because it may encourage the client to feel guilty about his behavior
    B. una*cceptable* cou*seling practice* , because the client may try to shock the counselor by confessing other similar behavior
    C. *acceptable counseling practice,* because "letting off steam" in this manner may relieve tension between the counselor and the client
    D. *unacceptable counseling practice,* because the client may hesitate to discuss his behavior frankly with the counselor in the future

16. During an interview, your client, who wants to move to a larger apartment, asks you to decide on a suitable neighborhood for her.
For you to make such a decision for the client would, generally, be considered

    A. *appropriate,* because you can save time and expense by sharing your knowledge of neighborhoods with the client
    B. *inappropriate,* because counselors should not help clients with this type of decision
    C. *appropriate,* because this will help the client to develop confidence in her ability to make decisions
    D. *inappropriate,* because the client should be encouraged to accept the responsibility of making this decision

16._____

17. A client tells you that he is extremely upset by the treatment that he received from Center personnel at the information desk.
Which of the following is the *BEST* way to handle this complaint during the interview?

    A. Explain to the client that he probably misinterpreted what occurred at the information desk
    B. Let the client express his feelings and then proceed with the interview
    C. Tell the client that you are not concerned with the personnel at the information desk
    D. Escort the client to the information desk to find out what really happened

17._____

18. You are finishing an interview with a client in which you have explained to her the procedure she must go through to apply for income maintenance.
Of the following, the *BEST* way for you to make sure that she has fully understood the procedure is to ask her

    A. whether she feels she has understood your explanation of the procedure
    B. whether she has any questions to ask you about the procedure
    C. to describe the procedure to you in her own words
    D. a few questions to test her understanding of the procedure

18._____

19. You are interviewing a client in his home as part of your investigation of an anonymous complaint that he has been receiving Medicaid fraudulently. During the interview, the client frequently interrupts your questions to discuss the hardships of his life and the bitterness he feels about his medical condition.
Of the following, the *BEST* way for you to deal with these discussions is to

    A. cut them off abruptly, since the client is probably just trying to avoid answering your questions
    B. listen patiently, since these discussions may be helpful to the client and may give you information for your investigation
    C. remind the client that you are investigating a complaint against him and he must answer directly
    D. seek to gain the client's confidence by discussing any personal or medical problems which you yourself may have

19._____

20. While interviewing an absent father to determine his ability to pay child supprt, you realize that his answers to some of your questions contradict his answers to other questions. Of the following, the BEST way for you to try to get accurate information from the father is to

   A. confront him with his contradictory answers and demand an explanation from him
   B. use your best judgment as to which of his answers are accurate and question him accordingly
   C. tell him that he has misunderstood your questions and that he must clarify his answers
   D. ask him the same questions in different words and follow up his answers with related questions

21. The one of the following types of interviewees who presents the LEAST difficult problem to handle is the person who

   A. answers with a great many qualifications
   B. talks at length about unrelated subjects so that the counselor cannot ask questions
   C. has difficulty understanding the counselor's vocabulary
   D. breaks into the middle of sentences and completes them with a meaning of his own

22. A man being interviewed is entitled to Medicaid, but he refuses to sign up for it because he says he cannot accept any form of welfare.
Of the following, the BEST course of action to take FIRST is to

   A. try to discover the reason for his feeling this way
   B. tell him that he should be glad financial help is available
   C. explain that others cannot help him if he will not help himself
   D. suggest that he speak to someone who is already on Medicaid

23. Of the following, the outcome of an interview by a counselor depends MOST heavily on the

   A. personality of the interviewee
   B. personality of the counselor
   C. subject matter of the questions asked
   D. interaction between counselor and interviewee.

24. Some clients being interviewed are primarily interested in making a favorable impression. The counselor should be aware of the fact that such clients are more likely than other clients to

   A. try to anticipate the answers the interviewer is looking for
   B. answer all questions openly and frankly
   C. try to assume the role of interviewer
   D. be anxious to get the interview over as quickly as possible

25. The type of interview which a counselor usually conducts is substantially different from most interviewing situations in all of the following aspects EXCEPT the

   A. setting
   B. kinds of clients
   C. techniques employed
   D. kinds of problems

KEY (CORRECT ANSWERS)

1.	A	11.	B
2.	A	12.	B
3.	B	13.	B
4.	D	14.	D
5.	A	15.	D
6.	D	16.	D
7.	D	17.	B
8.	A	18.	C
9.	B	19.	B
10.	A	20.	D

21. C
22. A
23. D
24. A
25. C

INTERVIEWING
EXAMINATION SECTION
TEST 1

DIRECTIONS: Each question or incomplete statement is followed by several suggested answers or completions. Select the one that BEST answers the question or completes the statement. *PRINT THE LETTER OF THE CORRECT ANSWER IN THE SPACE AT THE RIGHT.*

1. An interview is BEST conducted in private primarily because 1.____

   A. the person interviewed will tend to be less self-conscious
   B. the interviewer will be able to maintain his continuity of thought better
   C. it will insure that the interview is "off the record"
   D. people tend to "show off" before an audience

2. An interviewer can BEST establish a good relationship with the person being interviewed by 2.____

   A. assuming casual interest in the statements made by the person being interviewed
   B. taking the point of view of the person interviewed
   C. controlling the interview to a major extent
   D. showing a genuine interest in the person

3. An interviewer will be better able to understand the person interviewed and his problems if he recognizes that much of the person's behavior is due to motives 3.____

   A. which are deliberate
   B. of which he is unaware
   C. which are inexplicable
   D. which are kept under control

4. An interviewer's attention must be directed toward himself as well as toward the person interviewed. This statement means that the interviewer should 4.____

   A. keep in mind the extent to which his own prejudices may influence his judgment
   B. rationalize the statements made by the person interviewed
   C. gain the respect and confidence of the person interviewed
   D. avoid being too impersonal

5. More complete expression will be obtained from a person being interviewed if the interviewer can create the impression that 5.____

   A. the data secured will become part of a permanent record
   B. official information must be accurate in every detail
   C. it is the duty of the person interviewed to give accurate data
   D. the person interviewed is participating in a discussion of his own problems

6. The practice of asking leading questions should be avoided in an interview because the 6.____

   A. interviewer risks revealing his attitudes to the person being interviewed
   B. interviewer may be led to ignore the objective attitudes of the person interviewed
   C. answers may be unwarrantedly influenced
   D. person interviewed will resent the attempt to lead him and will be less cooperative

7. A good technique for the interviewer to use in an effort to secure reliable data and to reduce the possibility of misunderstanding is to

   A. use casual undirected conversation, enabling the person being interviewed to talk about himself, and thus secure the desired information
   B. adopt the procedure of using direct questions regularly
   C. extract the desired information from the person being interviewed by putting him on the defensive
   D. explain to the person being interviewed the information desired and the reason for needing it

8. You are interviewing a patient to determine whether she is eligible for medical assistance. Of the many questions that you have to ask her, some are routine questions that patients tend to answer willingly and easily. Other questions are more personal and some patients tend to resent being asked them and avoid answering them directly. For you to begin the interview with the more personal questions would be

   A. *desirable,* because the end of the interview will go smoothly and the patient will be left with a warm feeling
   B. *undesirable,* because the patient might not know the answers to the questions
   C. *desirable,* because you will be able to return to these questions later to verify the accuracy of the responses
   D. *undesirable,* because you might antagonize the patient before you have had a chance to establish rapport

9. While interviewing a patient about her family composition, the patient asks you whether you are married.
   Of the following, the MOST appropriate way for you to handle this situation is to

   A. answer the question briefly and redirect her back to the topic under discussion
   B. refrain from answering the question and proceed with the interview
   C. advise the patient that it is more important that she answer your questions than that you answer hers, and proceed with the interview
   D. promise the patient that you will answer her question later, in the hope that she will forget, and redirect her back to the topic under discussion

10. In response to a question about his employment history, a patient you are interviewing rambles and talks about unrelated matters.
    Of the following, the MOST appropriate course of action for you to take FIRST is to

    A. ask questions to direct the patient back to his employment history
    B. advise him to concentrate on your questions and not to discuss irrelevant information
    C. ask him why he is resisting a discussion of his employment history
    D. advise him that if you cannot get the information you need, he will not be eligible for medical assistance

11. Suppose that a person you are interviewing becomes angry at some of the questions you have asked, calls you meddlesome and nosy, and states that she will not answer those questions.
Of the following, which is the BEST action for you to take?

   A. Explain the reasons the questions are asked and the importance of the answers.
   B. Inform the interviewee that you are only doing your job and advise her that she should answer your questions or leave the office.
   C. Report to your supervisor what the interviewee called you and refuse to continue the interview.
   D. End the interview and tell the interviewee she will not be serviced by your department.

12. Suppose that during the course of an interview the interviewee demands in a very rude way that she be permitted to talk to your supervisor or someone in charge.
Which of the following is probably the BEST way to handle this situation?

   A. Inform your supervisor of the demand and ask her to speak to the interviewee.
   B. Pay no attention to the demands of the interviewee and continue the interview.
   C. Report to your supervisor and tell her to get another interviewer for this interviewee.
   D. Tell her you are the one "in charge" and that she should talk to you.

13. Of the following, the outcome of an interview by an aide depends MOST heavily on the

   A. personality of the interviewee
   B. personality of the aide
   C. subject matter of the questions asked
   D. interaction between aide and interviewee

14. Some patients being interviewed are primarily interested in making a favorable impression. The aide should be aware of the fact that such patients are more likely than other patients to

   A. try to anticipate the answers the interviewer is looking for
   B. answer all questions openly and frankly
   C. try to assume the role of interviewer
   D. be anxious to get the interview over as quickly as possible

15. The type of interview which an aide usually conducts is substantially different from most interviewing situations in all of the following aspects EXCEPT the

   A. setting   B. kinds of clients
   C. techniques employed D. kinds of problems

16. During an interview, an aide uses a "leading question." This type of question is so-called because it generally

   A. starts a series of questions about one topic
   B. suggests the answer which the aide wants
   C. forms the basis for a following "trick" question
   D. sets, at the beginning, the tone of the interview

17. Casework interviewing is always directed to the client and his situation. The one of the following which is the MOST accurate statement with respect to the proper focus of an interview is that the

   A. caseworker limits the client to concentration on objective data
   B. client is generally permitted to talk about facts and feelings with no direction from the caseworker
   C. main focus in casework interviews is on feelings rather than facts
   D. caseworker is responsible for helping the client focus on any material which seems to be related to his problems or difficulties

17.____

18. Assume that you are conducting a training program for the caseworkers under your supervision. At one of the sessions, you discuss the problem of interviewing a dull and stupid client who gives a slow and disconnected case history. The BEST of the following interviewing methods for you to recommend in such a case in order to ascertain the facts is for the caseworker to

   A. ask the client leading questions requiring "yes" or "no" answers
   B. request the client to limit his narration to the essential facts so that the interview can be kept as brief as possible
   C. review the story with the client, patiently asking simple questions
   D. tell the client that unless he is more cooperative he cannot be helped to solve his problem

18.____

19. A recent development in casework interviewing procedure, known as multiple-client interviewing, consists of interviews of the entire family at the same time. However, this may not be an effective casework method in certain situations. Of the following, the situation in which the standard individual interview would be preferable is when

   A. family members derive consistent and major gratification from assisting each other in their destructive responses
   B. there is a crucial family conflict to which the members are reacting
   C. the family is overwhelmed by interpersonal anxieties which have not been explored
   D. the worker wants to determine the pattern of family interaction to further his diagnostic understanding

19.____

20. A follow-up interview was arranged for an applicant in order that he could furnish certain requested evidence. At this follow-up interview, the applicant still fails to furnish the necessary evidence. It would be MOST advisable for you to

   A. advise the applicant that he is now considered ineligible
   B. ask the applicant how soon he can get the necessary evidence and set a date for another interview
   C. question the applicant carefully and thoroughly to determine if he has misrepresented or falsified any information
   D. set a date for another interview and tell the applicant to get the necessary evidence by that time.

20.____

KEY (CORRECT ANSWERS)

1.	A	11.	A
2.	D	12.	A
3.	B	13.	D
4.	A	14.	A
5.	D	15.	C
6.	C	16.	B
7.	D	17.	D
8.	D	18.	C
9.	A	19.	A
10.	A	20.	B

TEST 2

DIRECTIONS: Each question or incomplete statement is followed by several suggested answers or completions. Select the one that BEST answers the question or completes the statement. *PRINT THE LETTER OF THE CORRECT ANSWER IN THE SPACE AT THE RIGHT.*

1. In interviewing, the practice of anticipating an applicant's answers to questions is generally

   A. *desirable,* because it is effective and economical when it is necessary to interview large numbers of applicants
   B. *desirable,* because many applicants have language difficulties
   C. *undesirable,* because it is the inalienable right of every person to answer as he sees fit
   D. *undesirable,* because applicants may tend to agree with the answer proposed by the interviewer even when the answer is not entirely correct

2. When an initial interview is being conducted, one way of starting is to explain the purpose of the interview to the applicant. The practice of starting the interview with such an explanation is generally

   A. *desirable,* because the applicant can then understand why the interview is necessary and what will be accomplished by it
   B. *desirable,* because it creates the rapport which is necessary to successful interviewing
   C. *undesirable,* because time will be saved by starting directly with the questions which must be asked
   D. *undesirable,* because the interviewer should have the choice of starting an interview in any manner he prefers

3. For you to use responses such as "That's interesting," "Uh-huh" and "Good" during an interview with a patient is

   A. *desirable,* because they indicate that the investigator is attentive
   B. *undesirable,* because they are meaningless to the patient
   C. *desirable,* because the investigator is not supposed to talk excessively
   D. *undesirable,* because they tend to encourage the patient to speak freely

4. During the course of a routine interview, the BEST tone of voice for an interviewer to use is

   A. authoritative   B. uncertain
   C. formal   D. conversational

5. It is recommended that interviews which inquire into the personal background of an individual should be held in private. The BEST reason for this practice is that privacy

   A. allows the individual to talk freely about the details of his background
   B. induces contemplative thought on the part of the interviewed individual
   C. prevents any interruptions by departmental personnel during the interview
   D. most closely resembles the atmosphere of the individual's personal life

6. Assume that you are interviewing a patient to determine whether he has any savings accounts. To obtain this information, the MOST effective way to phrase your question would be:

   A. "You don't have any savings, do you?"
   B. "At which bank do you have a savings account?"
   C. "Do you have a savings account?"
   D. "May I assume that you have a savings account?"

7. You are interviewing a patient who is not cooperating to the extent necessary to get all required information. Therefore, you decide to be more forceful in your approach.
   In this situation, such a course of action is

   A. *advisable,* because such a change in approach may help to increase the patient's participation
   B. *advisable,* because you will be using your authority more effectively
   C. *inadvisable,* because you will not be able to change this approach if it doesn't produce results
   D. *inadvisable,* because an aggressive approach generally reduces the validity of the interview

8. You have attempted to interview a patient on two separate occasions, and both attempts were unsuccessful. The patient has been totally uncooperative and you sense a personal hostility toward you.
   Of the following, the BEST way to handle this type of situation would be to

   A. speak to the patient in a courteous manner and ask him to explain exactly what he dislikes about you
   B. inform the patient that you will not allow personality conflicts to disrupt the interview
   C. make no further attempt to interview the patient and recommend that he be billed in full
   D. discuss the problem with your supervisor and suggest that another investigator be assigned to try to interview the patient

9. At the beginning of an interview, a patient with normal vision tells you that he is reluctant to discuss his finances. You realize that it will be necessary in this case to ask detailed questions about his net income. When you begin this line of questioning, of the following, the LEAST important aspect you should consider is your

   A. precise wording of the question
   B. manner of questioning
   C. tone of voice
   D. facial expressions

10. A caseworker under your supervision has been assigned the task of interviewing a man who is applying for foster home placement for his two children. The caseworker seeks your advice as to how to question this man, stating that she finds the applicant to be a timid and self-conscious person who seems torn between the necessity of having to answer the worker's questions truthfully and the effect he thinks his answers will have on his application. Of the following, the BEST method for the caseworker to use in order to determine the essential facts in this case is to

A. assure the applicant that he need not worry since the majority of applications for foster home placement are approved
B. delay the applicant's narration of the facts important to the case until his embarrassment and fears have been overcome
C. ignore the statements made by the applicant and obtain all the required information from his friends and relatives
D. inform the applicant that all statements made by him will be verified and are subject to the law governing perjury

11. Assume that a worker is interviewing a boy in his assigned group in order to help him find a job. At the BEGINNING of the interview, the worker should

   A. suggest a possible job for the youth
   B. refer the youth to an employment agency
   C. discuss the youth's work history and skills with him
   D. refer the youth to the manpower and career development agency

12. As part of the investigation to locate an absent father, you make a field visit to interview one of the father's friends. Before beginning the interview, you identify yourself to the friend and show him your official identification.
For you to do this is, generally,

   A. *good practice,* because the friend will have proof that you are authorized to make such confidential investigations
   B. *poor practice,* because the friend may not answer your questions when he knows why you are interviewing him
   C. *good practice,* because your supervisor can confirm from the friend that you actually made the interview
   D. *poor practice,* because the friend may warn the absent father that your agency is looking for him

13. You are interviewing a client in his home as part of your investigation of an anonymous complaint that he has been receiving Medicaid fraudulently. During the interview, the client frequently interrupts your questions to discuss the hardships of his life and the bitterness he feels about his medical condition.
Of the following, the BEST way for you to deal with these discussions is to

   A. cut them off abruptly, since the client is probably just trying to avoid answering your questions
   B. listen patiently, since these discussions may be helpful to the client and may give you information for your investigation
   C. remind the client that you are investigating a complaint against him and he must answer directly
   D. seek to gain the client's confidence by discussing any personal or medical problems which you yourself may have

14. While interviewing an absent father to determine his ability to pay child support, you realize that his answers to some of your questions contradict his answers to other questions. Of the following, the BEST way for you to try to get accurate information from the father is to

   A. confront him with his contradictory answers and demand an explanation from him

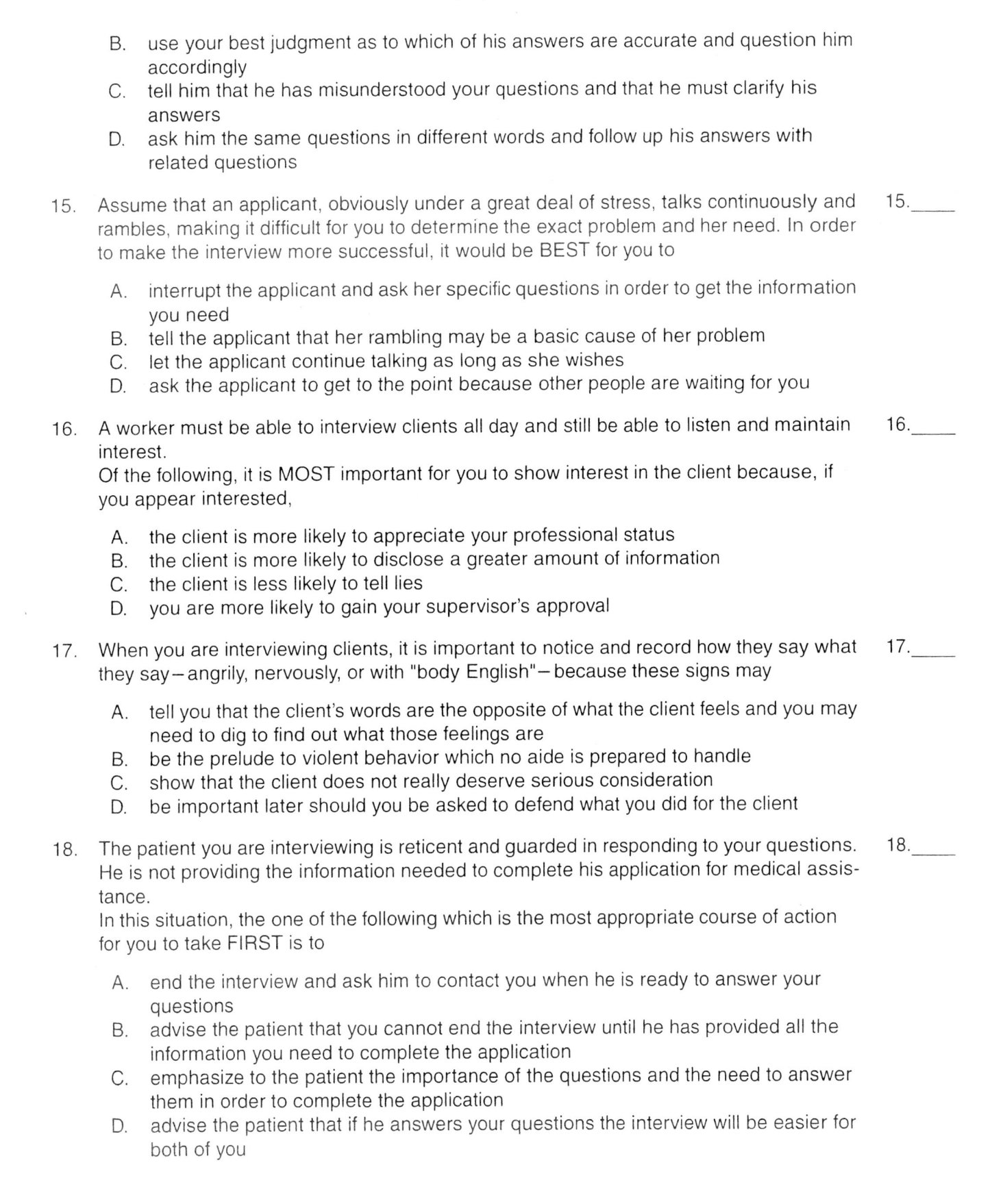

B. use your best judgment as to which of his answers are accurate and question him accordingly
C. tell him that he has misunderstood your questions and that he must clarify his answers
D. ask him the same questions in different words and follow up his answers with related questions

15. Assume that an applicant, obviously under a great deal of stress, talks continuously and rambles, making it difficult for you to determine the exact problem and her need. In order to make the interview more successful, it would be BEST for you to

    A. interrupt the applicant and ask her specific questions in order to get the information you need
    B. tell the applicant that her rambling may be a basic cause of her problem
    C. let the applicant continue talking as long as she wishes
    D. ask the applicant to get to the point because other people are waiting for you

16. A worker must be able to interview clients all day and still be able to listen and maintain interest.
    Of the following, it is MOST important for you to show interest in the client because, if you appear interested,

    A. the client is more likely to appreciate your professional status
    B. the client is more likely to disclose a greater amount of information
    C. the client is less likely to tell lies
    D. you are more likely to gain your supervisor's approval

17. When you are interviewing clients, it is important to notice and record how they say what they say—angrily, nervously, or with "body English"—because these signs may

    A. tell you that the client's words are the opposite of what the client feels and you may need to dig to find out what those feelings are
    B. be the prelude to violent behavior which no aide is prepared to handle
    C. show that the client does not really deserve serious consideration
    D. be important later should you be asked to defend what you did for the client

18. The patient you are interviewing is reticent and guarded in responding to your questions. He is not providing the information needed to complete his application for medical assistance.
    In this situation, the one of the following which is the most appropriate course of action for you to take FIRST is to

    A. end the interview and ask him to contact you when he is ready to answer your questions
    B. advise the patient that you cannot end the interview until he has provided all the information you need to complete the application
    C. emphasize to the patient the importance of the questions and the need to answer them in order to complete the application
    D. advise the patient that if he answers your questions the interview will be easier for both of you

19. At the end of an interview with a patient, he describes a problem he is having with his teenage son, who is often truant and may be using narcotics. The patient asks you for advice in handling his son.
Of the following, the MOST appropriate action for you to take is to

    A. make an appointment to see the patient and his son together
    B. give the patient a list of drug counseling programs to which he may refer his son
    C. suggest to the patient that his immediate concern should be his own hospitalization rather than his son's problem
    D. tell the patient that you are not qualified to assist him but will attempt to find out who can

19.____

20. A MOST appropriate condition in the use of direct questions to obtain personal data in an interview is that, whenever possible,

    A. the direct questions be used only as a means of encouraging the person interviewed to talk about himself
    B. provision be made for recording the information
    C. the direct questions be used only after all other methods have failed
    D. the person being interviewed understands the reason for requesting the information

20.____

KEY (CORRECT ANSWERS)

1.	D	11.	C
2.	A	12.	A
3.	A	13.	B
4.	D	14.	D
5.	A	15.	A
6.	B	16.	B
7.	A	17.	A
8.	D	18.	C
9.	A	19.	D
10.	B	20.	D

PREPARING WRITTEN MATERIAL

PARAGRAPH REARRANGEMENT
COMMENTARY

The sentences which follow are in scrambled order. You are to rearrange them in proper order and indicate the letter choice containing the correct answer at the space at the right.

Each group of sentences in this section is actually a paragraph presented in scrambled order. Each sentence in the group has a place in that paragraph; no sentence is to be left out. You are to read each group of sentences and decide upon the best order in which to put the sentences so as to form as well-organized paragraph.

The questions in this section measure the ability to solve a problem when all the facts relevant to its solution are not given.

More specifically, certain positions of responsibility and authority require the employee to discover connections between events sometimes, apparently, unrelated. In order to do this, the employee will find it necessary to correctly infer that unspecified events have probably occurred or are likely to occur. This ability becomes especially important when action must be taken on incomplete information.

Accordingly, these questions require competitors to choose among several suggested alternatives, each of which presents a different sequential arrangement of the events. Competitors must choose the MOST logical of the suggested sequences.

In order to do so, they may be required to draw on general knowledge to infer missing concepts or events that are essential to sequencing the given events. Competitors should be careful to infer only what is essential to the sequence. The plausibility of the wrong alternatives will always require the inclusion of unlikely events or of additional chains of events which are NOT essential to sequencing the given events.

It's very important to remember that you are looking for the best of the four possible choices, and that the best choice of all may not even be one of the answers you're given to choose from.

There is no one right way to these problems. Many people have found it helpful to first write out the order of the sentences, as they would have arranged them, on their scrap paper before looking at the possible answers. If their optimum answer is there, this can save them some time. If it isn't, this method can still give insight into solving the problem. Others find it most helpful to just go through each of the possible choices, contrasting each as they go along. You should use whatever method feels comfortable, and works, for you.

While most of these types of questions are not that difficult, we've added a higher percentage of the difficult type, just to give you more practice. Usually there are only one or two questions on this section that contain such subtle distinctions that you're unable to answer confidently, and you then may find yourself stuck deciding between two possible choices, neither of which you're sure about.

EXAMINATION SECTION
TEST 1

DIRECTIONS: The sentences that follow are in scrambled order. You are to rearrange them in proper order and indicate the letter choice containing the correct answer. *PRINT THE LETTER OF THE CORRECT ANSWER IN THE SPACE AT THE RIGHT.*

1. Below are four statements labeled W., X., Y., and Z.
    W. He was a strict and fanatic drillmaster.
    X. The word is always used in a derogatory sense and generally shows resentment and anger on the part of the user.
    Y. It is from the name of this Frenchman that we derive our English word, martinet.
    Z. Jean Martinet was the Inspector-General of Infantry during the reign of King Louis XIV.
   The *PROPER* order in which these sentences should be placed in a paragraph is:

   A. X, Z, W, Y   B. X, Z, Y, W   C. Z, W, Y, X   D. Z, Y, W, X

1.____

2. In the following paragraph, the sentences which are numbered, have been jumbled.
    1. Since then it has undergone changes.
    2. It was incorporated in 1955 under the laws of the State of New York.
    3. Its primary purpose, a cleaner city, has, however, remained the same.
    4. The Citizens Committee works in cooperation with the Mayor's Inter-departmental Committee for a Clean City.
   The order in which these sentences should be arranged to form a well-organized paragraph is:

   A. 2, 4, 1, 3   B. 3, 4, 1, 2   C. 4, 2, 1, 3   D. 4, 3, 2, 1

2.____

Questions 3-5.

DIRECTIONS: The sentences listed below are part of a meaningful paragraph but they are not given in their proper order. You are to decide what would be the *best order* in which to put the sentences so as to form a well-organized paragraph. Each sentence has a place in the paragraph; there are no extra sentences. You are then to answer questions 3 to 5 inclusive on the basis of your rearrangements of these secrambled sentences into a properly organized paragraph.

In 1887 some insurance companies organized an Inspection Department to advise their clients on all phases of fire prevention and protection. Probably this has been due to the smaller annual fire losses in Great Britain than in the United States. It tests various fire prevention devices and appliances and determines manufacturing hazards and their safeguards. Fire research began earlier in the United States and is more advanced than in Great Britain. Later they established a laboratory specializing in electrical, mechanical, hydraulic, and chemical fields.

3. When the five sentences are arranged in proper order, the paragraph starts with the sentence which begins

    A. "In 1887 ..."   B. "Probably this ..."   C. "It tests ..."
    D. "Fire research ..."   E. "Later they ..."

3.____

4. In the last sentence listed above, "they" refers to

    A. insurance companies
    B. the United States and Great Britain
    C. the Inspection Department
    D. clients
    E. technicians

4.____

5. When the above paragraph is properly arranged, it ends with the words

    A. "... and protection."   B. "... the United States."
    C. "... their safeguards."   D. "... in Great Britain."
    E. "... chemical fields."

5.____

KEY (CORRECT ANSWERS)

1. C
2. C
3. D
4. A
5. C

TEST 2

DIRECTIONS: In each of the questions numbered 1 through 5, several sentences are given. For each question, choose as your answer the group of numbers that represents the *most logical* order of these sentences if they were arranged in paragraph form. *PRINT THE LETTER OF THE CORRECT ANSWER IN THE SPACE AT THE RIGHT.*

1. 1. It is established when one shows that the landlord has prevented the tenant's enjoyment of his interest in the property leased.
    2. Constructive eviction is the result of a breach of the covenant of quiet enjoyment implied in all leases.
    3. In some parts of the United States, it is not complete until the tenant vacates within a reasonable time.
    4. Generally, the acts must be of such serious and permanent character as to deny the tenant the enjoyment of his possessing rights.
    5. In this event, upon abandonment of the premises, the tenant's liability for that ceases.

    The CORRECT answer is:

    A. 2, 1, 4, 3, 5   B. 5, 2, 3, 1, 4   C. 4, 3, 1, 2, 5
    D. 1, 3, 5, 4, 2

2. 1. The powerlessness before private and public authorities that is the typical experience of the slum tenant is reminiscent of the situation of blue-collar workers all through the nineteenth century.
    2. Similarly, in recent years, this chapter of history has been reopened by anti-poverty groups which have attempted to organize slum tenants to enable them to bargain collectively with their landlords about the conditions of their tenancies.
    3. It is familiar history that many of the workers remedied their condition by joining together and presenting their demands collectively.
    4. Like the workers, tenants are forced by the conditions of modern life into substantial dependence on these who possess great political arid economic power.
    5. What's more, the very fact of dependence coupled with an absence of education and self-confidence makes them hesitant and unable to stand up for what they need from those in power.

    The CORRECT answer is:

    A. 5, 4, 1, 2, 3   B. 2, 3, 1, 5, 4   C. 3, 1, 5, 4, 2
    D. 1, 4, 5, 3, 2

3. 1. A railroad, for example, when not acting as a common carrier may contract; away responsibility for its own negligence.
    2. As to a landlord, however, no decision has been found relating to the legal effect of a clause shifting the statutory duty of repair to the tenant.
    3. The courts have not passed on the validity of clauses relieving the landlord of this duty and liability.
    4. They have, however, upheld the validity of exculpatory clauses in other types of contracts.
    5. Housing regulations impose a duty upon the landlord to maintain leased premises in safe condition.

6. As another example, a bailee may limit his liability except for gross negligence, willful acts, or fraud.

The CORRECT answer is:

A. 2, 1, 6, 4, 3, 5   B. 1, 3, 4, 5, 6, 2   C. 3, 5, 1, 4, 2, 6
D. 5, 3, 4, 1, 6, 2

4.
1. Since there are only samples in the building, retail or consumer sales are generally eschewed by mart occupants, and, in some instances, rigid controls are maintained to limit entrance to the mart only to those persons engaged in retailing.
2. Since World War I, in many larger cities, there has developed a new type of property, called the mart building.
3. It can, therefore, be used by wholesalers and jobbers for the display of sample merchandise.
4. This type of building is most frequently a multi-storied, finished interior property which is a cross between a retail arcade and a loft building.
5. This limitation enables the mart occupants to ship the orders from another location after the retailer or dealer makes his selection from the samples.

The CORRECT answer is:

A. 2, 4, 3, 1, 5   B. 4, 3, 5, 1, 2   C. 1, 3, 2, 4, 5
D. 1, 4, 2, 3, 5

4.____

5.
1. In general, staff-line friction reduces the distinctive contribution of staff personnel.
2. The conflicts, however, introduce an uncontrolled element into the managerial system.
3. On the other hand, the natural resistance of the line to staff innovations probably usefully restrains over-eager efforts to apply untested procedures on a large scale.
4. Under such conditions, it is difficult to know when valuable ideas are being sacrificed.
5. The relatively weak position of staff, requiring accommodation to the line, tends to restrict their ability to engage .in free, experimental innovation.

The CORRECT answer is:

A. 4, 2, 3, 1, 3   B. 1, 5, 3, 2, 4   C. 5, 3, 1, 2, 4
D. 2, 1, 4, 5, 3

5.____

KEY (CORRECT ANSWERS)

1. A
2. D
3. D
4. A
5. B

TEST 3

DIRECTIONS: Questions 1 through 4 consist of six sentences which can be arranged in a logical sequence. For each question, select the choice which places the numbered sentences in the *most logical* sequence. *PRINT THE LETTER OF THE CORRECT ANSWER IN THE SPACE AT THE RIGHT.*

1. 1. The burden of proof as to each issue is determined before trial and remains upon the same party throughout the trial.
    2. The jury is at liberty to believe one witness' testimony as against a number of contradictory witnesses.
    3. In a civil case, the party bearing the burden of proof is required to prove his contention by a fair preponderance of the evidence.
    4. However, it must be noted that a fair preponderance of evidence does not necessarily mean a greater number of witnesses.
    5. The burden of proof is the burden which rests upon one of the parties to an action to persuade the trier of the facts, generally the jury, that a proposition he asserts is true.
    6. If the evidence is equally balanced, or if it leaves the jury in such doubt as to be unable to decide the controversy either way, judgment must be given against the party upon whom the burden of proof rests.

    The CORRECT answer is:

    A. 3, 2, 5, 4, 1, 6   B. 1, 2, 6, 5, 3, 4   C. 3, 4, 5, 1, 2, 6
    D. 5, 1, 3, 6, 4, 2

1.____

2. 1. If a parent is without assets and is unemployed, he cannot be convicted of the crime of non-support of a child.
    2. The term "sufficient ability" has been held to mean sufficient financial ability.
    3. It does not matter if his unemployment is by choice or unavoidable circumstances.
    4. If he fails to take any steps at all, he may be liable to prosecution for endangering the welfare of a child.
    5. Under the penal law, a parent is responsible for the support of his minor child only if the parent is "of sufficient ability."
    6. An indigent parent may meet his obligation by borrowing money or by seeking aid under the provisions of the Social Welfare Law.

    The CORRECT answer is:

    A. 6, 1, 5, 3, 2, 4   B. 1, 3, 5, 2, 4, 6   C. 5, 2, 1, 3, 6, 4
    D. 1, 6, 4, 5, 2, 3

2.____

3. 1. Consider, for example, the case of a rabble rouser who urges a group of twenty people to go out and break the windows of a nearby factory.
   2. Therefore, the law fills the indicated gap with the crime of inciting to riot."
   3. A person is considered guilty of inciting to riot when he urges ten or more persons to engage in tumultuous and violent conduct of a kind likely to create public alarm.
   4. However, if he has not obtained the cooperation of at least four people, he cannot be charged with unlawful assembly.
   5. The charge of inciting to riot was added to the law to cover types of conduct which cannot be classified as either the crime of "riot" or the crime of "unlawful assembly."
   6. If he acquires the acquiescence of at least four of them, he is guilty of unlawful assembly even if the project does not materialize.

   The CORRECT answer is:

   A. 3, 5, 1, 6, 4, 2
   B. 5, 1, 4, 6, 2, 3
   C. 3, 4, 1, 5, 2, 6
   D. 5, 1, 4, 6, 3, 2

4. 1. If, however, the rebuttal evidence presents an issue of credibility, it is for the jury to determine whether the presumption has, in fact, been destroyed.
   2. Once sufficient evidence to the contrary is introduced, the presumption disappears from the trial.
   3. The effect of a presumption is to place the burden upon the adversary to come forward with evidence to rebut the presumption.
   4. When a presumption is overcome and ceases to exist in the case, the fact or facts which gave rise to the presumption still remain.
   5. Whether a presumption has been overcome is ordinarily a question for the court.
   6. Such information may furnish a basis for a logical inference.

   The CORRECT answer is:

   A. 4, 6, 2, 5, 1, 3
   B. 3, 2, 5, 1, 4, 6
   C. 5, 3, 6, 4, 2, 1
   D. 5, 4, 1, 2, 6, 3

KEY (CORRECT ANSWERS)

1. D
2. C
3. A
4. B

PREPARING WRITTEN MATERIALS

EXAMINATION SECTION
TEST 1

DIRECTIONS: Each question consists of a sentence which may be classified appropriately under one of the following four categories:
- A. Incorrect because of faulty grammar or sentence structure;
- B. Incorrect because of faulty punctuation;
- C. Incorrect because of faulty capitalization;
- D. Correct.

Examine each sentence carefully. Then, in the space at the right, indicate the letter preceding the category which is the BEST of the four suggested above. Each incorrect sentence contains only one type of error. Consider a sentence correct if it contains no errors, although there may be other correct ways of expressing the same thought.

1. All the employees, in this office, are over twenty-one years old. 1.____

2. Neither the clerk nor the stenographer was able to explain what had happened. 2.____

3. Mr. Johnson did not know who he would assign to type the order. 3.____

4. Mr. Marshall called her to report for work on Saturday. 4.____

5. He might of arrived on time if the train had not been delayed. 5.____

6. Some employees on the other hand, are required to fill out these forms every month. 6.____

7. The supervisor issued special instructions to his subordinates to prevent their making errors. 7.____

8. Our supervisor Mr. Williams, expects to be promoted in about two weeks. 8.____

9. We were informed that prof. Morgan would attend the conference. 9.____

10. The clerks were assigned to the old building; the stenographers, to the new building. 10.____

11. The supervisor asked Mr. Smith and I to complete the work as quickly as possible. 11.____

12. He said, that before an employee can be permitted to leave, the report must be finished. 12.____

13. An adding machine, in addition to the three typewriters, are needed in the new office. 13.____

14. Having made many errors in her work, the supervisor asked the typist to be more careful. 14.____

15. "If you are given an assignment," he said, "you should begin work on it as quickly as possible." 15.____

16. All the clerks, including those who have been appointed recently are required to work on the new assignment. 16.____

17. The office manager asked each employee to work one Saturday a month. 17.____

18. Neither Mr. Smith nor Mr. Jones was able to finish his assignment on time. 18.____

19. The task of filing these cards is to be divided equally between you and he. 19.____

20. He is an employee whom we consider to be efficient. 20.____

21. I believe that the new employees are not as punctual as us. 21.____

22. The employees, working in this office, are to be congratulated for their work. 22.____

23. The delay in preparing the report was caused, in his opinion, by the lack of proper supervision and coordination. 23.____

24. John Jones accidentally pushed the wrong button and then all the lights went out. 24.____

25. The investigator ought to of had the witness sign the statement. 25.____

KEY (CORRECT ANSWERS)

1. B
2. D
3. A
4. C
5. A

6. B
7. D
8. B
9. C
10. D

11. A
12. B
13. A
14. A
15. D

16. B
17. C
18. D
19. A
20. D

21. A
22. B
23. D
24. D
25. A

TEST 2

Questions 1-10.

DIRECTIONS: Each of the following sentences may be classified under one of the following four options:
- A. Faulty; contains an error in grammar only
- B. Faulty; contains an error in spelling only
- C. Faulty; contains an error in grammar and an error in spelling
- D. Correct; contains no error in grammar or in spelling

Examine each sentence carefully to determine under which of the above four options it is BEST classified. Then, in the space at the right, write the letter preceding the option which is the best of the four listed above.

1. A recognized principle of good management is that an assignment should be given to whomever is best qualified to carry it out.   1.____

2. He considered it a privilege to be allowed to review and summarize the technical reports issued annually by your agency.   2.____

3. Because the warehouse was in an inaccessable location, deliveries of electric fixtures from the warehouse were made only in large lots.   3.____

4. Having requisitioned the office supplies, Miss Brown returned to her desk and resumed the computation of petty cash disbursements.   4.____

5. One of the advantages of this chemical solution is that records treated with it are not inflamable.   5.____

6. The complaint of this employee, in addition to the complaints of the other employees, were submitted to the grievance committee.   6.____

7. A study of the duties and responsibilities of each of the various categories of employees was conducted by an unprejudiced classification analyst.   7.____

8. Ties of friendship with this subordinate compels him to withold the censure that the subordinate deserves.   8.____

9. Neither of the agencies are affected by the decision to institute a program for rehabilitating physically handi-caped men and women.   9.____

10. The chairman stated that the argument between you and he was creating an intolerable situation.   10.____

Questions 11-25.

DIRECTIONS: Each of the following sentences may be classified under one of the following four options:

A. Correct
B. Sentence contains an error in spelling
C. Sentence contains an error in grammar
D. Sentence contains errors in both grammar and spelling.

11. He reported that he had had a really good time during his vacation although the farm was located in a very inaccessible portion of the country. 11.____

12. It looks to me like he has been fasinated by that beautiful painting. 12.____

13. We have permitted these kind of pencils to accumulate on our shelves, knowing we can sell them at a profit of five cents apiece any time we choose. 13.____

14. Believing that you will want an unexagerated estimate of the amount of business we can expect, I have made every effort to secure accurate figures. 14.____

15. Each and every man, woman and child in that untrameled wilderness carry guns for protection against the wild animals. 15.____

16. Although this process is different than the one to which he is accustomed, a good chemist will have no trouble. 16.____

17. Insensible to the fuming and fretting going on about him, the engineer continued to drive the mammoth dynamo to its utmost capacity. 17.____

18. Everyone had studied his lesson carefully and was consequently well prepared when the instructor began to discuss the fourth dimention. 18.____

19. I learned Johnny six new arithmetic problems this afternoon. 19.____

20. Athletics is urged by our most prominent citizens as the pursuit which will enable the younger generation to achieve that ideal of education, a sound mind in a sound body. 20.____

21. He did not see whoever was at the door very clearly but thinks it was the city tax appraiser. 21.____

22. He could not scarsely believe that his theories had been substantiated in this convincing fashion. 22.____

23. Although you have displayed great ingenuity in carrying out your assignments, the choice for the position still lies among Brown and Smith. 23.____

24. If they had have pleaded at the time that Smith was an accessory to the crime, it would have lessened the punishment. 24.____

25. It has proven indispensible in his compilation of the facts in the matter. 25.____

KEY (CORRECT ANSWERS)

1.	A		11.	A
2.	D		12.	D
3.	B		13.	C
4.	D		14.	B
5.	B		15.	D
6.	A		16.	C
7.	D		17.	A
8.	C		18.	B
9.	C		19.	C
10.	A		20.	A

21.	B
22.	D
23.	C
24.	D
25.	B

TEST 3

Questions 1-5.

DIRECTIONS: Questions 1 through 5 consist of sentences which may or may not contain errors in grammar or spelling or both. Sentences which do not contain errors in grammar or spelling or both are to be considered correct, even though there may be other correct ways of expressing the same thought. Examine each sentence carefully. Then, in the space at the right, write the letter of the answer which is the BEST of those suggested below:
- A. If the sentence is correct;
- B. If the sentence contains an error in spelling;
- C. If the sentence contains an error in grammar;
- D. If the sentence contains errors in both grammar and spelling.

1. Brown is doing fine although the work is irrevelant to his training. 1.____

2. The conference of sales managers voted to set its adjournment at one o'clock in order to give those present an opportunity to get rid of all merchandise. 2.____

3. He decided that in view of what had taken place at the hotel that he ought to stay and thank the benificent stranger who had rescued him from an embarassing situation. 3.____

4. Since you object to me criticizing your letter, I have no alternative but to consider you a mercenary scoundrel. 4.____

5. I rushed home ahead of schedule so that you will leave me go to the picnic with Mary. 5.____

Questions 6-15.

DIRECTIONS: Some of the following sentences contain an error in spelling, word usage, or sentence structure, or punctuation. Some sentences are correct as they stand although there may be other correct ways of expressing the same thought. All incorrect sentences contain only one error. Mark your answer to each question in the space at the right as follows:
- A. If the sentence has an error in spelling;
- B. If the sentence has an error in punctuation or capitalization;
- C. If the sentence has an error in word usage or sentence structure;
- D. If the sentence is correct.

6. Because the chairman failed to keep the participants from wandering off into irrelevant discussions, it was impossible to reach a consensus before the meeting was adjourned. 6.____

7. Certain employers have an unwritten rule that any applicant, who is over 55 years of age, is automatically excluded from consideration for any position whatsoever. 7.____

8. If the proposal to build schools in some new apartment buildings were to be accepted by the builders, one of the advantages that could be expected to result would be better communication between teachers and parents of schoolchildren. 8.____

9. In this instance, the manufacturer's violation of the law against deseptive packaging was discernible only to an experienced inspector. 9.____

10. The tenants' anger stemmed from the president's going to Washington to testify without consulting them first. 10.____

11. Did the president of this eminent banking company say; "We intend to hire and train a number of these disadvan-taged youths?" 11.____

12. In addition, today's confidential secretary must be knowledgable in many different areas: for example, she must know modern techniques for making travel arrangements for the executive. 12.____

13. To avoid further disruption of work in the offices, the protesters were forbidden from entering the building unless they had special passes. 13.____

14. A valuable secondary result of our training conferences is the opportunities afforded for management to observe the reactions of the participants. 14.____

15. Of the two proposals submitted by the committee, the first one is the best. 15.____

Questions 16-25.

DIRECTIONS: Each of the following sentences may be classified MOST appropriately under one of the following three categories:
    A. Faulty because of incorrect grammar
    B. Faulty because of incorrect punctuation
    C. Correct

Examine each sentence. Then, print the capital letter preceding the BEST choice of the three suggested above. All incorrect sentences contain only one type of error. Consider a sentence correct if it contains none of the types of errors mentioned, even though there may be other ways of expressing the same thought.

16. He sent the notice to the clerk who you hired yesterday. 16.____

17. It must be admitted, however that you were not informed of this change. 17.____

18. Only the employees who have served in this grade for at least two years are eligible for promotion. 18.____

19. The work was divided equally between she and Mary. 19.____

20. He thought that you were not available at that time. 20.____

21. When the messenger returns; please give him this package. 21.____

22. The new secretary prepared, typed, addressed, and delivered, the notices. 22.____

23. Walking into the room, his desk can be seen at the rear. 23.____

24. Although John has worked here longer than she, he produces a smaller amount of work. 24.____

25. She said she could of typed this report yesterday. 25.____

KEY (CORRECT ANSWERS)

1. D
2. A
3. D
4. C
5. C

6. A
7. B
8. D
9. A
10. D

11. B
12. A
13. C
14. D
15. C

16. A
17. B
18. C
19. A
20. C

21. B
22. B
23. A
24. C
25. A

TEST 4

Questions 1-5.

DIRECTIONS: Each of the following sentences may be classified MOST appropriately under one of the following three categories:
    A. Faulty because of incorrect grammar
    B. Faulty because of incorrect punctuation
    C. Correct

Examine each sentence. Then, print the capital letter preceding the BEST choice of the three suggested above. All incorrect sentences contain only one type of error. Consider a sentence correct if it contains none of the types of errors mentioned, even though there may be other correct ways of expressing the same thought.

1. Neither one of these procedures are adequate for the efficient performance of this task.   1.____
2. The typewriter is the tool of the typist; the cash register, the tool of the cashier.   2.____
3. "The assignment must be completed as soon as possible" said the supervisor.   3.____
4. As you know, office handbooks are issued to all new employees.   4.____
5. Writing a speech is sometimes easier than to deliver it before an audience.   5.____

Questions 6-15.

DIRECTIONS: Each statement given in Questions 6 through 15 contains one of the faults of English usage listed below. For each, choose from the options listed the MAJOR fault contained.
    A. The statement is not a complete sentence.
    B. The statement contains a word or phrase that is redundant.
    C. The statement contains a long, less commonly used word when a shorter, more direct word would be acceptable.
    D. The statement contains a colloquial expression that normally is avoided in business writing.

6. The fact that this activity will afford an opportunity to meet your group.   6.____
7. Do you think that the two groups can join together for next month's meeting?   7.____
8. This is one of the most exciting new innovations to be introduced into our college.   8.____
9. We expect to consummate the agenda before the meeting ends tomorrow at noon.   9.____
10. While this seminar room is small in size, we think we can use it.   10.____
11. Do you think you can make a modification in the date of the Budget Committee meeting?   11.____
12. We are cognizant of the problem but we think we can ameliorate the situation.   12.____
13. Shall I call you around three on the day I arrive in the City?   13.____

14. Until such time that we know precisely that the students will be present. 14.____

15. The consensus of opinion of all the members present is reported in the minutes. 15.____

Questions 16-25.

DIRECTIONS: For each of Questions 16 through 25, select from the options given below the MOST applicable choice.
    A. The sentence is correct.
    B. The sentence contains a spelling error only.
    C. The sentence contains an English grammar error only.
    D. The sentence contains both a spelling error and an English grammar error.

16. Every person in the group is going to do his share. 16.____

17. The man who we selected is new to this University. 17.____

18. She is the older of the four secretaries on the two staffs that are to be combined. 18.____

19. The decision has to be made between him and I. 19.____

20. One of the volunteers are too young for this complecated task, don't you think? 20.____

21. I think your idea is splindid and it will improve this report considerably. 21.____

22. Do you think this is an exagerated account of the behavior you and me observed this morning? 22.____

23. Our supervisor has a clear idea of excelence. 23.____

24. How many occurences were verified by the observers? 24.____

25. We must complete the typing of the draft of the questionaire by noon tomorrow. 25.____

KEY (CORRECT ANSWERS)

1.	A		11.	C
2.	C		12.	C
3.	B		13.	D
4.	C		14.	A
5.	A		15.	B
6.	A		16.	A
7.	B		17.	C
8.	B		18.	C
9.	C		19.	C
10.	B		20.	D

21. B
22. D
23. B
24. B
25. B

BASIC FUNDAMENTALS OF INTERVIEWING AND COUNSELING

TABLE OF CONTENTS

	Page
I. INTRODUCTION	1
II. PRESENTATION	1
A. The Art of Interviewing	1
B. Types of Interviews	1
1. Classified by Purpose	1
2. Classified by Method	2
3. Classified by Technique	3
C. How to Conduct Interviews	3
1. Preparing for the Interview	3
2. Conducting the Interview	3
3. Closing the Interview	4
D. The Counseling Interview	5
1. Purpose of Counseling Interviews	5
2. The Supervisor as a Counselor	5
E. Interview Checklist	5
III. SUMMARY	6
Sample Questions	7
Interviewing and Counseling – Outlines 1-5	8

INTERVIEWING AND COUNSELLING

I. Introduction

For this unit our objectives are limited. Both interviewing and counselling have been, and are now, the subjects of extensive study. Advances in knowledge in these fields occul from day-to-day. All that we can hope to accomplish is to give you an overview that will help you to more effectively use the interview, including the counselling interview, in meeting your supervisory responsibilities. We will discuss, generally, what an interview is, the various types of interviews, and how to conduct interviews.

Our objectives are to provide you with: (1) an understanding of the art of interviewing, (2) knowledge of the uses of interviews, and (3) knowledge of techniques for successfully conducting interviews and counselling.

II. Presentation

A. The Art of Interviewing

Interviewing is an art. It is more than a systematized body of knowledge. To be a successful interviewer, one has to develop skill in handling an interview situation. Because the interview takes place between two or more human beings, highly individualized, with differing emotional responses, no set of rules can be applicable at all times in all situations. It is the discernment of the right approach to any given interview situation which gives rise to the art.

You are not strangers to interviewing. You have all been interviewed at one time or another. It is probably safe to say that all of you have conducted interviews. Having been on both sides of the interviewing situation, you have recognized that the emotional responses of the interviewer and interviewee differ. You have, perhaps, felt that if the person interviewing you knew what he was doing you would derive more from the interview. Or while interviewing, you may have wondered how the interview got out of hand, or why the interviewee reacted as he did. If so, you may have become aware of the fact that an interview involves a subtler relationship between human beings than is commonly supposed.

What, then, is an interview? It is a purposeful, directed conversation between two or more people. It is not an aimless conversation. It has a definite purpose, and the conversation is directed toward accomplishing that purpose. The person who takes the responsibility for the direction of the conversation is the interviewer.

What are the purposes for which interviews are intended? Generally speaking these purposes are: (1) to obtain information, (2) to give information, (3) to solve problems and (4) to influence the behavior of individuals. An interview may combine two or more purposes. To discuss these purposes more fully, let us look at the types of interviews.

B. *Types of Interviews*

1. *Classified By Purpose*

a. *Fact Finding Interviews*

This type of interview should be used discriminatingly. The kind of information that can be elicited by interviewing is not only of observable, objective facts of conditions or events, but also of subjective facts such as opinions, interpretations, and attitudes of the person interviewed. The objective facts are frequently discoverable by other means, but the subjective facts can be determined only from the individual involved.

When answers to questions can be obtained from records or documents, or by observation of situations, these answers are more reliable, and usually are obtainable more quickly, accurately and economically than by interviewing. However, even though this is so, you may still want to conduct fact finding interviews. For two reasons: (1) to secure subjective facts and (2) to secure additional leads that may provide access to more sources of objective data.

b. *Appraisal Interview*

The appraisal interview is an essential supervisory tool. More and more, supervisors are beginning to realize that "once a year is just not enough." Communication must take place as a continuing day-to-day process.

Real two-way communication between you and the employee cannot possibly be achieved in a mandatory, one-time, annual formal interview. Actually, the number of interviews with any one employee should vary according to individual needs. Whenever you become aware-for example, through an examination of regular work reports, by on-the-job observation, periodic review of work, spot check, etc.-that an employee's performance, good or poor, can profitably be discussed with him, that is the time to talk with him. In other words, the interviews should be carried on naturally, as occasions arise.

This type of interview is used with subordinates to: (1) let them know where they stand, (2) recognize their good work, (3) let them know how, and in what particulars they should improve, (4) develop them in their present jobs, (5) develop and train them for higher jobs, (6) set self-development goals, and (7) to warn borderline employees that they must improve and how.

c. *Error Correcting Interview*

This type of interview will be a frequent one in your supervisory life. Subordinates like everybody else will make mistakes. Possibly because of personal problems, inaptitude for the job, and even because they haven't been properly trained. Your job in such an interview is to determine the cause of the error so that you can help the subordinate to avoid repeating that error.

d. *Grievance Interview*

An employee comes to you with a complaint. You interview him to get the facts so that you may either resolve the problem or recommend action to your superiors. This type of interview has always been extremely important and often very difficult. It now has greater implications because of the Government's management-employee cooperation policy. A grievance interview not properly handled could result in magnifying a problem.

e. *The Counselling Intervieiv*

This interview is intended to help an employee help himself. Counselling is the process of talking things over with an employee who has a problem, in such a way that he will be helped to solve his difficulty and will be better able to cope with difficult situations in the future. Helping the employee solve his problems helps management to get more and better work from the employee.

2. *Classified by Method*

a. *Individual Interview*

The interviewer and interviewee alone are involved. This type of interview is most frequently used. It can be used for fact finding and grievances and should usually be used in appraisal, error correcting and counselling interviews.

b. *Group Interview*

One or more interviewers meet with a group of interviewees. This, too, may be used for all types of interview classified by purpose. It sometimes is more effective than the individual interview. Particularly, if you want to discover leadership ability, ability to get along with others and problem solving. By presenting a problem for discussion, the interviewer can observe the interaction of the group. Individuals will reveal a great deal of information about themselves by the way they conduct themselves in such a situation.

c. *Panel Interview*

A group or panel of interviewers meet with one interviewee. Here the individual members of the interviewing team have an opportunity to observe and evaluate personal characteristics of the interviewee, his ability to reason and to express himself clearly, his attitudes, his interests, and what he thinks of his abilities. This type of interview is not used to secure information which can be more accurately secured by other means. For example, IQ can be more accurately determined by appropriate tests. The panel interview is used to measure and evaluate characteristics which are not measurable by other means. As a matter of fact, the less the panel knows about the interviewee's IQ, test scores, educational background and previous experience, the more valid will be its evaluation.

   3. *Classified by Technique*
      a. *Directed*

   The directed or controlled interview is used to get facts. It is best described as the question and answer technique. This can be very effective where the interviewee is cooperative, is at ease, and is under no tension or apprehension.

      b. *Non-Structured*

   A free flowing interviewing technique used to get information without specifically asking for it. The interviewee is encouraged to talk about whatever it is he wants to talk about. Frequently, this type of interview will get quickly to the core of a problem. The interviewer doesn't have to probe with questions to try to determine what the problem is. This technique is effective in counselling, grievance and appraisal interviews.

C. *How to Conduct Interviews*
   1. *Preparing for the Interview*
      a. Decide your objective. What is it that you want to accomplish in the interview? Are you seeking facts? What facts specifically will you need? Are you trying to correct errors, alter behavior, or suggest to the interviewee how he can improve his work? Whatever your objectives, you should have them fixed firmly in your mind. You might write them down to keep as a ready reference while you conduct the interview. Many interviews fail to accomplish their purpose because the interviewer gets sidetracked from his objectives.

      b. Know the interviewee. Secure as much information as possible about the person to be interviewed. The more you know about him, the better you will be able to understand his motives, his responses, his frames of reference, and his ability to comprehend.

      c. Make appointments if at all possible. Setting aside a definite time to conduct the interview shows the interviewee that you are considerate of his time. You know that the hour is satisfactory to him. By having time allocated in your schedule, you don't waste your time or that of the interviewee.

      d. If possible, arrange for privacy. An interviewee will not be ready to confide in you if he can be overheard by others. Confidential matters or embarassing facts will be withheld if they are to become public knowledge.

      e. Put yourself in the interviewee's place. Try to take his point of view. How would you feel being interviewed by a person who has your traits, attitudes, and appearance. How would you expect to be treated if you had this or that problem. Having an idea of how the interviewee will react will help you to adjust the manner in which you conduct the interview so that you can accomplish your objectives.

      f. Study yourself. Try to know your own personality. Each of us is the sum total of his experiences. We have definite attitudes and prejudices. We are not often aware of this. But what we are does affect what we do and how we think. Too often we think in terms of stereotypes. We all know what a "criminal" looks like, don't we? In literature criminals are all shifty-eyed, beetle-browed, and weak-chinned. In real life, contrary to our stereotype image, they frequently have the face of an angel. We should try to know our prejudices, so that even if we can't get rid of them, at least we will not let them intrude in the interview situation.

   2. *Conducting the Interview*
      a. Establish mutual confidence. It is the interviewer's responsibility to set the tone for the interview. The interviewee must trust you and be willing to confide in you. You have to let him know that you trust him, too. You must show sincerity and must really be

sincere. Lack of sincerity is easily spotted and will destroy respect.

b. Establish pleasant associations. There is no need for the interviewer to ever lose his temper. One can be firm without being unpleasant. The interviewee may become angry, and, possibly, expressing his anger may be helpful, but still the interview should be as pleasant as possible.

c. Put the interviewee at ease. He will be more ready to talk if he is relaxed. A good way to put the interviewee at ease is to be at ease yourself. Encourage him to talk by letting him know that you believe his ideas are important and that you are interested in hearing them. Avoid the temptation to evaluate or judge his statements. He should be allowed to express his own ideas, unhampered by your ideas, your values and preconceptions.

d. Listen to what the interviewee says. You are interviewing him to find out what he thinks. You won't find that out listening to your own voice. To be a successful interviewer, one must learn to listen. He must listen not only to the words spoken, but must listen so that he understands what the interviewee is saying. The interviewee may not be able to express himself clearly, coherently or logically. The interviewer has to listen attentively to grasp the full meaning of what the interviewee is trying to say.

Listening is extremely important in all interviews, but is particularly important in grievance and counselling interviews. Often times, the mere fact that the interviewee has an attentive interviewer interested in what he is saying is enough to ameliorate the grievance. Just being able to "let off steam" may help the interviewee to see his grievance in better perspective. This is not a newly discovered psychological principle. The Vizier Ptah-Hotep, sometime between 2700 and 2200 B.C. gave this advice to his son: "If thou art one to whom petition is made, be calm as thou listenest to what the petitioner has to say. Do not rebuff him before he has swept out his body or before he has said that for which he came. The petitioner likes attention to his words better than the fulfilling of that for which he came ... It is not necessary that everything about which he has petitioned should come to pass, but a good hearing is soothing to the heart."

e. Allow enough time. You can ruin an interview by glancing at your watch. An interviewee is not going to be relaxed and communicative if he has to race the clock. The time allotted should be adequate to accomplish the objectives of the interview. A few minutes may be enough to handle some problems, while others may require several hours. Long interviews are exhausting. It is better, where you can, to limit the objectives, and schedule two or more sessions for the interview.

3. *Closing the Interview*

a. When to close. This is not always easy to determine. Circumstances vary both with the type of interview and the personality of the interviewee. With practice, an interviewer can develop an intuition for spotting the appropriate moment for closing the interview. If you have accomplished your interview objectives, or if it becomes apparent that you will not be able to accomplish them, you should bring the interview to a close. If you haven't been able to accomplish your interview objectives, agree on a definite future interview appointment with the interviewee. Nothing is gained by allowing a discussion to drag on. But you should not be abrupt in closing an interview. The interviewee should be assured by your words and manner of your interest and respect.

b. Consolidate your gains. Your windup of the interview should be a consolidation of the progress that has been made by the interview: you want the interviewee to leave knowing what has been accomplished. Also, you may avoid future misunderstandings with a good review. Your review should contain these elements:

    (1) A summary of the points covered
    (2) A statement of the agreements reached
    (3) A statement stressing the value of the interview
    (4) A statement of continuing interest on the part of the interviewer thus leaving the door open for future interviews.

    c. *The Natural Closing*

The closing of an interview should not be forced. You should not try to end all interviews alike. Be natural. The closing should not be in sharp contrast to the interview. In an interview where you had to admonish an employee, small talk at closing would be inappropriate.

Be sincere in your closing. An incidental "Oh, by the way, how's the family?" said at the door, will mark you as insincere.

A handshake is sometimes appropriate. But if it makes you feel uncomfortable or is inappropriate to the nature of the interview just concluded, then the handshake is out of place. Remember one rule, though, never refuse a handshake offered you.

  D. *The Counselling Interview*
    1. *Purpose of Counselling Interview*

The primary purpose of counselling is the better adjustment of the employee as a worker, resulting in a more satisfying work experience and increased productivity. Our purpose is to help the employee recognize his limitations, to vocalize his problems, and to assist him in deciding what course of action he can take to improve himself and increase his value to the organization or, sometimes, to accept himself or the situation and to live with it.

We are not trained psychotherapists. If you have any reason to suspect that the individual has a problem with disturbed psychic overtones, don't tamper with the individual. The problems of the human mind, the complexities of neurosis or psychosis are in the province of professional therapists. We have to avoid the temptation to make snap judgments of personality. The layman is eager to identify and categorize. He says "Joe, you have an inferiority complex." The trained psychologist, social worker, and psychiatrist will study the man intensely before making observations and then won't tell "Joe" about it. Remember, you can cause a lot of damage if you tamper with individuals whose problems are of a complex psychic nature.

    2. *The Supervisor as a Counsellor*

As a supervisor, you are the first level of management to receive the impact of problems from your subordinates. Your willingness to listen, your sincere interest in the problems of your employees, and your availability and approachability, will increase your potential as a supervisor.

The supervisor's role as a counsellor is one that he cannot avoid, nor should he want to. It gives him an opportunity to learn about his subordinates and what motivates them. It helps him build mutual confidence and respect. It removes barriers to growth. It provides a basis for cooperative effort. It helps to accomplish unit production goals.

  E. Interview Checklist

After every interview, you will do well to evaluate yourself as an interviewer. By studying your actions in each interview, you can benefit from your interviewing experience. What did you say or do that contributed to the success of the interview? What did you say or do that caused the interview to be unsuccessful? Your analysis will help to enhance your interviewing skill.

Check yourself against this list.

Yes No

1. Were you friendly?
   a. Did you really feel friendly?
   b. Was this friendliness communicated?
   c. Did the interviewee respond to your friendliness?
2. Were you interested in the interviewee as an individual?
3. Were you interested in his problem?
4. Did you prepare adequately for the interview?
5. Did you state your purpose as soon as possible?
6. Were you unhurried and relaxed?
7. Did the interviewee seem at ease?
8. Did you try to reduce his nervousness or fear?
9. Did you get him to say what was on his mind?
10. Did you give him enough time to talk?
11. Did you interrupt his explanations?
12. Did you disagree with him?
13. If you disagreed, were you pleasant about it?
14. Were your questions challenging or argumentative?
15. Did you listen to everything he said?
16. Was your attitude respectful?
17. Did you encourage him to give examples and to elaborate on unclear points?

Yes No

18. Did you invite him to ask questions or raise additional problems?
19. Did your gestures help convey your attitude?
20. Did you refrain from giving advice or lecturing?
21. Did you make any reference to your continued interest and willingness to help?
22. Did you answer his questions?
23. Did you summarize the gains made?
24. Did you close on a friendly note?
25. Do you have a plan for following-up the interview?

III. *Summary*

We have discussed the nature of interviewing and have seen that it is an art in which you can become skilled. We have discussed the various types of interview and have classified them by purpose, method and technique.

We have discussed how interviews should be conducted. We stressed the importance of preparing for an interview, suggested steps to follow in conducting the interview, and analyzed the closing of the interview. Together, we looked at the nature of the counselling interview and saw that, for our purposes, it concerns normal problems of normal people. We saw that the sole objective of the counselling interview is to lead the interviewee to a clear understanding of his problem so that he realizes what action to take and assumes responsibility for taking it.

We then reviewed a checklist that you may use to evaluate your interviewing ability.

Remember, how successful an interviewer you become depends entirely on you.

INTERVIEWING AND COUNSELLING

Sample Questions

1. *Question.* What are the purposes of interviews?
   Answer. To obtain information, to give information, to solve problems, to influence behavior.

2. *Question.* How does a panel interview differ from a group interview?
   Answer. A panel interview: More than one interviewer, only one interviewee. A group interview: One or more interviewers, and more than one interviewee.

3. *Question.* When is a directed interview effective?
   Answer. When the interviewee is cooperative, is relaxed, and is under no tension or apprehension.

4. *Question.* What is the non-structured approach?
   Answer. It is a free flowing interviewing technique in which the interviewee is encouraged to talk about what he wants to.

5. *Question.* How should you prepare for an interview?
   Answer. Determine your objectives, know the interviewee, make a definite appointment, arrange for privacy, put yourself in interviewee's place, study yourself.

6. *Question.* What should you remember in conducting an interview?
   Answer. To establish mutual confidence, to establish pleasant associations, to put the interviewee at ease, to listen, and to allow enough time.

7. *Question.* How should you close the interview?
   Answer. Close at the appropriate point, consolidate your gains, and use a natural closing.

8. *Question.* How does counselling help the employee?
   Answer. Helps employee understand the obstacles to his future growth and development, helps employee to recognize his limitations, helps him vocalize his problems, assists him in solving his problems.

9. *Question.* How does counselling help the supervisor?
   Answer. It gives him opportunity to learn what motivates his subordinates, it helps build mutual confidence and respect, releases potential of employees, improves cooperation, and helps achieve production goals.

OUTLINE 1

INTERVIEWING AND COUNSELLING

Interviews—Classified by Purpose
    Fact Finding Interviews
        —To secure subjective facts
        —To secure additional leads that may provide access to more sources of objective data
    Appraisal Interview
        —To let employee know where he stands
        —To recognize good work
        —To let employee know how, and in what particulars, he should improve
        —To develop employees in present jobs
        —To develop and train them for higher jobs
        —To set self-development goals
        —To warn borderline employees that they must improve and how
    Error Correcting Interview
        —To determine cause of errors
        —To help employee to avoid repetition of errors
    Grievance Interview
        —To afford aggrieved employee opportunity to be heard
        —To collect information
        —To act on grievance either directly or by recommending action to your superiors
    Counselling Interview
        —To help employee solve his personal problems
        —To improve morale
        —To improve production
        —To improve work habits

OUTLINE 2

INTERVIEWING AND COUNSELLING

Interviews—Classified by Method
   Individual Interview
      —One interviewer and one interviewee alone are involved
      —Used for fact-finding, appraisal, error correcting, grievances and counselling
   Group Interview
      —One or more interviewers meet with a group of interviewees
      —Useful in observing individual reactions in a group situation. Exposes leadership ability, ability to get along with others and ability to solve problems
   Panel Interview
      —A group or panel of interviewers meet with one interviewee
      —Used to observe and evaluate personal characteristics of interviewee, his ability to reason and express himself clearly, his attitudes, his interests, and what he thinks of his abilities

Interviews—Classified by Technique
   Directed Interview
      —Used to get facts
      —Direct questioning is used
      —Is effective where interviewee is cooperative, relaxed, and is under no tension or apprehension
   Non-Structured Interview
      —Free flowing technique used to get information without specifically asking for it
      —Interviewee is encouraged to talk about whatever he wants to talk about
      —The interviewer does not probe—he listens
      —This technique is effective in counselling, grievances and appraisal interviews

OUTLINE 3
INTERVIEWING AND COUNSELLING

How to Conduct Interviews
  Preparing for the Interview
    a. Decide what the objective or objectives of this interview will be
    b. Know the interviewee
    c. Make a definite appointment for the interview
    d. Arrange for a place of privacy to conduct the interview
    e. Put yourself in the interviewee's place
    f. Study yourself
  Conducting the Interview
    a. Establish mutual confidence
    b. Establish pleasant associations
    c. Put the interviewee at ease
    d. Listen to what the interviewee says
    e. Allow enough time
  Closing the Interview
    a. Close at the appropriate point. Don't cut interview short—don't drag it out
    b. Consolidate your gains by:
      —Summarizing the points covered
      —Restating the agreements reached
      —Stressing the value of this interview
      —Expressing continued interest and leaving the door open for future interview
    c. The natural closing
      —Don't force it
      —Be natural
      —Be sincere

OUTLINE 4
INTERVIEWING AND COUNSELLING

The Counselling Interview
    Purpose of Counselling Interview
- To help the employee understand the obstacles to further growth and development that are typified by his specific difficulty
- To help the employee to recognize his limitations
- To help him vocalize his problems
- To assist him in deciding what course of action to take
- To deal with the normal problems of normal people

    The Supervisor as a Counsellor
- A role you cannot avoid, nor should you want to
- You learn what motivates your subordinates
- You build mutual confidence and respect
- You remove barriers to growth
- You improve cooperation
- You increase probability of accomplishing unit production goals

OUTLINE 5

INTERVIEWING AND COUNSELLING
Interview Checklist

		Yes	No
1.	Were you friendly?		
	a. Did you really feel friendly?		
	b. Was this friendliness communicated?		
	c. Did the interviewee respond to your friendliness?		
2.	Were you interested in the interviewee as an individual?		
3.	Were you interested in his problem?		
4.	Did you prepare adequately for the interview?		
5.	Did you state your purpose as soon as possible?		
6.	Were you unhurried and relaxed?		
7.	Did the interviewee seem at ease?		
8.	Did you try to reduce his nervousness or fear?		
9.	Did you get him to say what was on his mind?		
10.	Did you give him enough time to talk?		
11.	Did you interrupt his explanations?		
12.	Did you disagree with him?		
13.	If you disagreed, were you pleasant about it?		
14.	Were your questions challenging or argumentative?		
15.	Did you listen to everything he said?		
16.	Was your attitude respectful?		
17.	Did you encourage him to give examples and to elaborate on unclear points?		
18.	Did you invite him to ask questions or raise additional problems?		
19.	Did your gestures help convey your attitude?		
20.	Did you refrain from giving advice or lecturing?		
21.	Did you make any reference to your continued interest and willingness to help?		
22.	Did you answer his questions?		
23.	Did you summarize the gains made?		
24.	Did you close on a friendly note?		
25.	Do you have a plan for following-up the interview?		

COUNSELING THE ALCOHOLIC

CONTENTS

I. PHILOSOPHY AND PRINCIPLES	1
II. THREE STAGES OF RELATIONSHIP	1
III. THE INITIAL INTERVIEW	2
IV. THE CONTINUING RELATIONSHIP	4
V. GROUP COUNSELING	5
VI. GROUP THERAPY AND A. A.	7

COUNSELING THE ALCOHOLIC

I. PHILOSOPHY AND PRINCIPLES

The alcoholic who is not ready to undergo treatment will often protest,. "Only an alcoholic can help an alcoholic!"

That is not true.

But the counselor -- alcoholic or non-alcoholic --who would help the man or woman whose life is disintegrating because of drinking should thoroughly understand the physical and emotional pain involved before attempting to establish rapport.

The essential quality is one of empathy, which the dictionary defines as "the capacity for participating in another's feelings or ideas." It differs from sympathy in that the counselor does not become emotionally involved, allowing the patient's joys and sorrows to affect his own ability to evaluate and advise.

The effective counselor must not only be able to understand others. He must have a real desire to understand others, to explore the whys of human behavior. And he must have an unconditional, positive regard for the individual patient -- a blend of warmth, acceptance, regard, interest, and respect.

He must continually work on his own self-awareness. He should recognize his own hang-ups and learn to deal with them. One who is able to do this is better able to be a partner in a helping relationship.

He must always remember that he is a counselor, not an analyst nor a judge. Overconcern with personality theories and counseling techniques will endanger rapport, just as premature attempts to arrive at solutions will surely lead to the patient's being short-changed.

Equipped with a knowledge of the physiological and psychological nature of alcoholism and especially of its progressive symptoms, the trained counselor usually is in a position to assess the general status of the new patient who sits before him. He has a broad idea of the physical pains, emotional distress, and changing attitudes the alcoholic has already suffered. This may be a small start. But it is an important head start in winning acceptance and evolving a program for recovery.

From that point on it is the counselor's job to translate his general observations into full and meaningful particulars about the highly individual person who seeks his help. Once that is accomplished, they can work together towards reasonable decisions and practical steps to be taken.

II. THREE STAGES OF RELATIONSHIP

Effective relationships between alcoholism counselors and their patients can be broken down into three stages:

The first might be called the subjective period. During this, usually the initial interview, the counselor wins the patient's confidence and establishes his empathy with him. He then gathers as much pertinent information as possible -- e.g., personal data, marriage and family status, employment, hospitalizations and arrests, drinking habits, etc.

The second is an objective stage. The counselor points out to the patient his current status in comparison with known patterns and established facts about the disease. He explains what could lie ahead.

The third stage is one of teamwork. The counselor joins with the patient in building a road to recovery and solving the problems still posed by the past.

III. THE INITIAL INTERVIEW

   A. Importance

The initial interview usually is the most important, not only because "first impressions" tend to linger on, but because it may also be the last.

For a variety of reasons, the counselor may never again set eyes upon his patient. One of the most common -- particularly in outpatient clinics -- is that the patient is not sufficiently motivated to undergo continuing treatment. At the moment, the prospect of a lifetime without drinking is too frightening. He should nevertheless leave the counselor's office knowing that the door will always be open to him, tomorrow or ten years hence.

A sense of security is the key to gaining the new patient's confidence so that he will come back.

So the patient must be satisfied that the counselor will respect whatever confidences he may choose to divulge. He must be reasonably confident that the counselor is not going to berate him as he has been berated in the past. He must be assured that he can lower his defenses and receive understanding instead of recrimination.

The counselor cannot expect to be told pertinent confidences unless the patient has confidence in him.

   B. The Contract

Also in the initial interview, a "contract" should be established.

The patient must be aware that alcoholism is an illness -- not a sin or a sign of weakness of character. Whether or not he is suffering from that illness will be up to him to decide, if he has not already done so.

If the answer is yes, he has two choices: to accept treatment or to continue drinking. If he chooses the latter, probably, eventually, it will result in custodial care or death.

However, if he sincerely wants to recover, he must accept the fact that he is a sick man who can no longer drink. The counselor and his colleagues cannot do this for him. But they can help him help himself.

Such are the essentials of the initial contract. The counselor can make them clear in any way that best befits the situation or the patient's general attitude at the time. But unless the patient subscribes to them, any recovery program is courting failure.

C. Eliciting Patient History

The primary concern in a counselor-patient relationship is "Where do we go from here?" But significant facts about the patient's past and present are necessary for any reliable estimate of the situation.

In the course of time, counselors develop their individual methods of eliciting this information. So it would be presumptuous here to advance any hard-and-fast rules about interviewing new patients as one would instruct a student in the operation of a computer. However, there are certain basic principles to be considered.

The truism that "the quality of the answer depends upon the quality of the question" is universally accepted. The patient must be made to feel that he has the interviewer's undivided attention. He can perceive the presence or lack of empathy not only by the questions asked, but also by the counselor's overall manner. The tone of voice can be more persuasive than the questions themselves. Questions that reflect accusation and suspicion on the part of the counselor arouse resentment and suspicion in the patient and can quickly erase whatever rapport has been established in the beginning.

Even the pacing should be adjusted to the patient. Too slow a pace may suggest a difficulty in understanding on the part of the counselor. Too fast a pace can imply lack of interest.

Some questions must of necessity be pointed and direct e.g., date of birth, marital status, employment, etc. Those are to be expected. Other pointed questions - such as those dealing with the patient's parental and childhood background - are more readily answered if the purpose in asking them is explained. But,in general, pithy questions are preferable to those that can be answered yes or no. They can lead to greater insight into the patient's personality.

D. Problems and Solutions

Then there is the question that slams the door. The patient "clams up." More often than not it touches upon a painful memory which triggers the frigid reaction. It is useless to pursue the point at that time. The counselor can come back to it later in the interview or, as often happens, the patient will inadvertently supply the answer while responding to another evocative question.

In the same category are evasions and obvious lies. Few alcoholics will admit to having more than "a couple of beers" before their accidents, arrests,or other plights. The first meeting is no time to break down their defenses. Usually "the truth will out" -- that the patient had a pint and a half of whiskey between the two beers -- before the interview is over. The counselor should accept both the lie and its disproval without comment. The same holds true for other camouflages thrown up by the patient.

Nor are all answers verbal. The counselor should listen to what the patient does not say, as well as to what he says. The omissions in his explanations and comments are frequently more revealing than the explanations themselves. At the same time, physical clues can also be expressive of the emotional attitude -- e.g., the sweaty palms arising from fear or a sense of guilt, the folded arms of contrariness, the tears of sheer frustration and self-pity.

The most empathic alcoholism counselor in the world could not hope for a perfect batting average among all the applicants who come to him for aid. Perfect rapport cannot be arranged by an admission desk. Sometimes a patient might better be counseled by a worker in the next room or one down the hall. Or he may gravitate to a new group leader, even after weeks of individual counseling by the person who first interviewed him. In such cases, the counselor should have no hesitancy in "letting the patient go."

E. Problems that the Counselor Cannot Solve

The counselor must be able to distinguish between the patients he can help and those he cannot. He should recognize his own capabilities and limitations. It may be that a difficult family or financial situation or some other involved personal problem is causing or substantially contributing to the patient's drinking. When it is apparent that the cause, whatever it may be, is beyond the counselor's ability to help, he should refer the patient to an agency which can.

IV. THE CONTINUING RELATIONSHIP

Most of the above observations also apply to the continuing counselor-patient relationship. Of course, once the ice has been broken in the initial interviews and confidence established, the alcoholic is not apt to revert to lies and evasions with his counselor or physician. If he has normal intelligence, he will have found out that frankness best paves the way for significant planning and decisions.

Nor are there any precise ground rules to guide the counselor in an ongoing relationship. Success lies in adapting himself to the patient's attitude and, through empathy, helping him to plan ways and means of reaching the goals he sincerely wants to reach. In other words, the counselor has to "play it by ear."

A. Basics

But there are several basic "rules of thumb."

In planning ways and means of reaching objectives, final decisions should be made by the patient, not by the counselor.

One must remember that the average alcoholic comes glutted with unasked-for advice -- opinionated guidance supplied by family, parents, employer, best friend, and well-meaning companions. The patient is tired of advice.

So even if the counselor should know the answers, he should forego the role of mastermind. Better he discuss the pros and cons until the patient can view himself and his situation in the cold light of reality and decide for himself what had best be done to remedy matters. This is not to say that the counselor cannot offer alternatives, nor should he allow the patient to decide upon a potentially disastrous course of action. But when the patient himself makes the final decision or believes that he made it -- it becomes a strictly personal matter. It is no longer advice from family, parents, employer, or best friend. It is his own decision and, as such, he has greater confidence in the chances for success, especially with the counselor and his resources to lend support.

   B.   <u>Constructive Forces</u>

Besides being surfeited with advice, the average alcoholic comes oppressed with feelings of guilt and inferiority and loss of self-respect. The counselor should search out the constructive forces in his client. He must believe in them and their potentialities. And then he must make the patient realize them and believe in them, too. He can always cite the truism that every man is superior to the next man in some respect -- physically, psychologically, or intellectually. Once that asset is recognized, it can become another steppingstone in planning the road to recovery.

One of the beneficial by-products of counseling is catharsis the process by which repressed emotions and memories are brought to consciousness and released. It is an outpouring of emotionally painful thoughts which the patient has been harboring inside himself with perhaps no one available to console or consult, and which he has futile-ly been attempting to drown in drink. The counselor-patient relationship offers an opportunity for such purgative relief.

Catharsis should be fostered, but not forced. As he listens, the counselor should be alert to responses by the patient which reflect feeling rather than mere recollection, emotions rather than intellect. Strongly felt sentiments can reveal themselves at almost any time e.g., while talking about the family's reaction to his drinking, difficulties on the job, strained relation in the community. The bald recital of an occurrence may impulsively be punctuated with the patient's emotional reaction to the event. This is the time for the counselor to encourage him to express his feelings instead of just facts. But his questions and comments should be leading rather than probing, persuasive rather than pressing. Otherwise the patient may crawl back into his private world and slam the door behind him.

V.   GROUP COUNSELING

As a general rule alcoholics are more effectively treated in group therapy than in the traditional one-to-one counselor-patient relationship.

This does not mean that the patient's need for individual counseling is completely superseded when he becomes a member of a group. Strictly personal problems may arise. Help from outside resources may be needed. Periods of uncertainty and depression may threaten his new self-command. In such cases, he may need individual counseling for support.

But for ongoing therapy the group affords a climate which the alcoholic has been avoiding for months or even years. Hiding his drinking habits from others or protecting his supply, he has usually become a loner. As participant in a group, he again becomes a member of society a society in miniature, perhaps, but nevertheless, a cooperative body with common aims and interests. It evokes intercommunication and, hopefully, interaction with others so necessary in again facing up to reality and normal living.

This escape from isolation is only one of many benefits a patient can derive from group therapy. The interpersonal relationships with others faced with the same illness gradually reduces his own sensitivity. He finds understanding, reassurance, and support. As time goes on, he gains greater insight into the origins and evolution of his behavior patterns. He is re-educated in ways of adapting himself to reality. And, because the environment is real, not artificial, he can test many of those ways within the group itself.

A. <u>Role of the Group Leader</u>

The group leader -- be he alcoholism counselor, social worker, or psychiatrist -- must always remember that the group belongs to its members. His primary mission is to be a good listener, with any outward participation kept to a minimum. The members must feel that they are the ones who are choosing the questions for discussion, arriving at the answers, settling any conflicts or confrontations.

However passive his role may appear to be, the leader must see to it that the discussion does not wander too far away from the subject. He should encourage participation by the silent minority, if any. He should act to relieve tensions and mediate debates. And, at all times, he should be noting the actions and reactions of the individual members, for these are clues to their progress in the recovery program.

While all these duties might seem to conflict with the leader's role as passive observer, he can usually delegate action to others.

Every group is made up of as many different personalities as there are members. They unconsciouly tend to assume various roles which they continue to play week after week. The leader can usually count upon them to function as needed. Among them are: The
- Initiator--introduces new ideas or subjects for discussion.
- Information-seeker -- asks for pertinent facts.
- Information-giver, -- always ready to supply those pertinent facts if he can.
- Elaborator -- develops others' comments and ideas.
- Orienter -- raises questions about the direction of discussion.
- Coordinator -- tries to pull ideas and suggestions together.
- Tester -- checks whether the group is ready for decision.
- Opinion-giver -- states what he believes to be the consensus of the group.
- Such members -- and other members in other roles -- are the group leader's advocates.

B. <u>Measuring the Success of the Group</u>

Superficially, it might seem easiest to measure the success of any group by the faithful attendance of its members and its attraction of new members.

But the true effectiveness of a group is best reflected in its contribution to its members' recovery. From time to time, the leader should ask himself these questions:

Has our group created an atmosphere in which constructive progress can be made?

Has it achieved real communication among members?

Do the members freely give and freely receive help?

Are the conditions such that each member can make his own special contribution?

Does it allow conflict and confrontation to be resolved into creative problem solving?

Has it evolved acceptable ways of making decisions?

If the leader can answer yes to all of these questions, he and the group are accomplishing their mission. If not, he had better diagnose the shortcomings and repair them.

VI. GROUP THERAPY AND A.A.

One frequently hears Alcoholics Anonymous vaguely referred to as "group psychotherapy."

In reality, there are many basic differences between the two methods of treatment. But a layman's misunderstanding can be forgiven since both have one aim among others -- to help the alcoholic stop drinking.

The counselor should be aware of these differences because the confusion is a common one.

A. <u>Differences Between the Two Methods</u>

In balancing method, it is best to disregard A.A.'s open meetings, where the general public is invited to attend, and limit comparisons to A.A.'s closed meetings, for alcoholics only.

Both A.A. and clinical groups are open to all alcoholics regardless of race, sex, or socio-economic status. While the latter are deliberately kept heterogeneous, members of A.A. tend to gravitate to groups composed of racial and socio-economic peers.

Both stress confidentiality. Outside visitors are not allowed. A.A. closed meetings do not permit the non-alcoholic spouses of members to attend. Clinical groups, recognizing alcoholism as a family disease, urge participation by members' families.

So long as alcoholic patients are under clinical treatment, they are required to attend group meetings, which are usually limited in size -- preferably six to nine participants. A.A. members are not required to attend meetings. Nor are there any limitations as to size. Hence, the same group can vary greatly from week to week in both numbers and make-up.

Leadership in clinical groups is vested in a trained psychotherapist or alcoholism counselor who unobtrusively steers discussion, mediates differences, and, when called upon, answers pertinent questions concerning alcohol and alcoholism. A.A. groups are presided over by a chairman, usually selected weekly on a rotating basis. The only requirement is to be an abstaining alcoholic.

The cornerstone of A.A. therapy is belief in a "God as one understands Him" and reliance upon His power to effect "a spiritual awakening" which will support a new, continuing life without alcohol. Catharsis and reparation for past wrongs committed against others are intended to alleviate guilt. Identification with other members who have succeeded in the program is stressed. Abstinence is the goal.

Clinical therapy, on the other hand, centers on psychological aspects. The alcoholic's nonrational and fantastic life theme is brought out and, through inter-communication and interaction with other group members, is eventually accepted by the patient and hopefully altered. The strengthening of relationships with other group members develops a sense of responsibility both for himself and for others. Full sobriety, not merely abstinence, is the goal.

In A.A., life membership is encouraged for continuing support. In clinical therapy, the successful member eventually leaves the group and stands on his own.

There are other differences, but these are the basic ones. The two therapies do not contravene one another. For many patients, they complement each other. When such is the case, the alcoholic can profitably embrace both.

ANSWER SHEET

TEST NO. _____ PART _____ TITLE OF POSITION _____
(AS GIVEN IN EXAMINATION ANNOUNCEMENT - INCLUDE OPTION, IF ANY)

PLACE OF EXAMINATION _____ _____ DATE _____
(CITY OR TOWN) (STATE)

RATING

USE THE SPECIAL PENCIL. MAKE GLOSSY BLACK MARKS.

Make only ONE mark for each answer. Additional and stray marks may be counted as mistakes. In making corrections, erase errors COMPLETELY.

ANSWER SHEET

MAY - - 2017

TEST NO. _____ PART _____ TITLE OF POSITION _____
(AS GIVEN IN EXAMINATION ANNOUNCEMENT - INCLUDE OPTION, IF ANY)

PLACE OF EXAMINATION _____ DATE _____
(CITY OR TOWN)   (STATE)

RATING

USE THE SPECIAL PENCIL.   MAKE GLOSSY BLACK MARKS.

Make only ONE mark for each answer.   Additional and stray marks may be counted as mistakes.   In making corrections, erase errors COMPLETELY.